FLIP-IT-OVER
GUIDES TO TEEN EMOTIONS

A Girls' Guide to

Conflict

Dorothy Kavanaugh

Enslow Publishers, Inc.
40 Industrial Road
Box 398
Berkeley Heights, NJ 07922
USA

http://www.enslow.com

Library of Congress Cataloging-in-Publication Data

Gallagher, Jim, 1969- A guys' guide to conflict ; A girls' guide to conflict / Jim Gallagher and Dorothy Kavanaugh.
 p. cm. — (Flip-it-over guides to teen emotions)
 No collective t.p.; titles transcribed from individual title pages.
 Includes bibliographical references and index.
 ISBN-13: 978-0-7660-2852-4
 ISBN-10: 0-7660-2852-6
 1. Conflict management—Juvenile literature. 2. Boys—Life skills guides—Juvenile literature.
3. Girls—Life skills guides—Juvenile literature. I. Gallagher, Jim, 1969- Guy's guide to conflict.
II. Title. III. Title: Guys' guide to conflict.

 HM1126.C38 2008
 303.6'9—dc22

                          2007026457

Printed in the United States of America.

10 9 8 7 6 5 4 3 2 1

Produced by OTTN Publishing, Stockton, NJ.

To Our Readers: We have done our best to make sure all Internet Addresses in this book were active and appropriate when we went to press. However, the author and the publisher have no control over and assume no liability for the material available on those Internet sites or on other Web sites they may link to. Any comments or suggestions can be sent by e-mail to comments@enslow.com or to the address on the title page.

Photo Credits: © Barbara Spitzer/PhotoEdit, p. 1; Corbis Images, pp. 11, 28; Illustration by JimHunt.us, pp. 4, 9 (Easel), 20; ImageState, p. 35; © iStockphoto.com/Jim Pruitt, p. 16; © iStockphoto.com/Michael Gatewood, p. 52; © John Bavosi/Photo Researchers, Inc., p. 9 (Brain); © John Birdsall/Visuals Unlimited, p. 57 (top); © 2007 Jupiterimages Corporation, pp. 27, 34, 45; © Peter Byron/PhotoEdit, p. 47; PhotoDisc, Inc., p. 55; Used Under License from Shutterstock, Inc., pp. 3, 13, 15, 30, 38, 50, 57 (bottom).

Cover Photo: © Barbara Spitzer/PhotoEdit

CONTENTS

CHAPTER ONE

Conflict and Your Emotions

Disagreement. Strife. Friction. Quarrel. Dispute. All of these words are synonyms for conflict. Although the word *conflict* can be used to describe a wide range of situations, it usually boils down to not seeing or understanding someone else's point of view.

Conflict is part of everyone's life. You can feel conflict inside yourself, for example, whenever you have to choose between something you *want* to do and something you *have* to do. And there are times when you have conflict with others—such as when a friend accuses you of lying or your parents criticize your report card. Conflicts also occur because of disagreements and differences between groups—in ideas, opinions, values, beliefs, lifestyles, and personalities.

Being hassled on the school bus can unleash a storm of emotions.

Conflict can cause a range of powerful emotions. When two girls harassed fifteen-year-old Leslie during a school bus ride home, she felt humiliated.

"I could hear two of the older girls whispering and laughing at me," she explained. "I could feel my face get red and I tried to read my book and ignore them. The next thing I knew they were throwing spitballs and everyone was laughing."[1]

Conflicts Can Occur...

- **In society**: among people with different values, religions, and ethnic groups
- **In your personal relationships**: with family, friends, and teachers
- **Within yourself**: when you have to make a hard decision or you learn something different from your previous beliefs

But Leslie felt many other emotions as well:

> *I was angry with the girls, and with everyone else, for laughing and being so mean when I didn't deserve it. I think that I was also angry with myself for not having the courage to stand up to them. But I was very afraid of them also, they were bigger and older. . . . I was totally embarrassed because it was obvious that I was not going to stand up to these girls. I was also actually surprised at the depth of their cruelty.*[2]

When you have a conflict with another person, it is normal to feel angry, frustrated, disappointed, or sad. However, sometimes people in a conflict allow their emotions to control their actions, and they react in destructive ways. They might yell and swear at the other person. Some will lash out or get into fights. This kind of behavior makes it hard to work things out.

You may think conflict is bad. After all, fights and disagreements are often uncomfortable and unpleasant. But conflict is neither negative nor positive. It is simply the meeting of two or more different needs, feelings, or expectations. The way that a conflict is managed is what determines whether it is "good" or "bad."

In Leslie's case, she handled her conflict through avoidance. That is, she decided to avoid her tormentors by no longer riding the bus. Sometimes avoidance may be the only appropriate solution, especially when dealing directly with harassment is not safe. Avoidance kept Leslie out of harm's way, but it did not address the conflict. If she had shared her problem with someone else, such as the bus driver, it is possible she could have resolved the problem in a better way.

Not directly addressing this conflict affected Leslie in the years that followed. "The bus ride incident has always stuck with me," she admits. "Those girls made me feel terrible about

You and Your Emotions

A part of everyone's personality, emotions are a powerful driving force in life. They are hard to define and understand. But what is known is that emotions—which include anger, fear, love, joy, jealousy, and hate—are a normal part of the human system. They are responses to situations and events that trigger bodily changes, motivating you to take some kind of action.

Some studies show that the brain relies more on emotions than on intellect in learning and in making decisions. Being able to identify and understand the emotions in yourself and in others can help you in your relationships with family, friends, and others throughout your life.

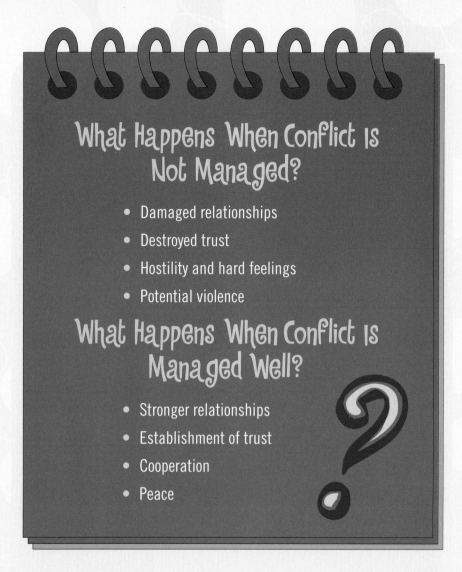

What Happens When Conflict Is Not Managed?

- Damaged relationships
- Destroyed trust
- Hostility and hard feelings
- Potential violence

What Happens When Conflict Is Managed Well?

- Stronger relationships
- Establishment of trust
- Cooperation
- Peace

myself, and shook up my self-confidence quite a bit. . . . I felt like a real failure."[3]

Conflict can overwhelm some teens to the point that they engage in dangerous or harmful behaviors to release their emotions. Such behaviors include violence, drug or alcohol abuse, self-mutilation (cutting), and even thoughts of suicide.

This book gives you positive ways to deal with conflicts you will experience in life, both as a young person and as an adult. Its tips and strategies can help you learn positive ways to control your emotions, avoid fights, and resolve conflicts.

CHAPTER TWO

Your Brain Under Conflict

Conflict becomes a bigger part of life during your teen years. That's when you are developing the values, opinions, and personalities that will determine what you will be like as an adult.

Right now, you are beginning to examine and weigh the values that your parents and community have taught you. And you are deciding which of these beliefs and opinions to keep and which to reject. This weighing process is totally normal. It, along with your natural drive toward independence, helps you develop self-identity. However, your search for values, testing of opinions, and testing of boundaries can also contribute to a lot of conflict—both within you and within your family.

There are also biological reasons why emotions are powerful during the teen years. One reason is that the brain is undergoing great change. For a long time scientists have known that the brain's basic structure is shaped during the first few years of an infant's life. What researchers have recently learned is that a second period of significant change begins around the time a person hits puberty—a time when the rest of the body is also going through many changes.

During puberty the amygdala—a part of the lower brain that regulates emotions—becomes more dominant. This change

Puberty refers to the time when a young person's body is developing and changing as she becomes an adult. In girls, puberty usually starts between ages eight and thirteen.

Science Says....

The amygdala is all about survival. It sends signals to the rest of the brain, causing the body to take immediate, unthinking reactions when faced with a threat. This response is known as the "fight-or-flight" instinct. That is, the body is strengthened as it prepares to defend itself from danger or run away from it. The fight-or-flight response has ensured the survival of individuals since prehistoric times, when people faced wild animals or other enemies.

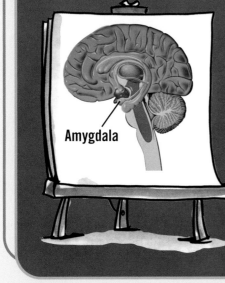

Amygdala

This survival response still kicks in today whenever people encounter conflict and become angry. They feel a rush of adrenaline and, often, an increased feeling of confidence that enables them to confront the source of their anger.

The amygdala regulates emotions like fear, anger, and anxiety.

means that a teen can have strong swings in emotion, which can affect her judgments and decision-making. As the teenage girl gets older, the frontal lobes of her brain develop further. In an adult, this area, which controls reasoning and judgment, takes over much of the amygdala's role.

A second reason for higher levels of conflict among teenagers is also a result of puberty. During this time, the

The Female Brain

Louann Brizendine is a neuropsychiatrist who believes that young boys and girls behave differently because their brains are different. In her book *The Female Brain*,[1] Brizendine states that the centers in girls' brains that control language, communication, and the observation and expression of emotions are bigger than the same centers in boys' brains. Because young girls are better "wired" to connect with others, Brizendine says, they tend to promote social harmony, and minimize or avoid conflict. According to Brizendine, biological differences in the brains of boys mean they are more likely to be confrontational in conflicts.

Science journalist Robin Marantz Henig disagrees. She says that there are differences in male and female behavior because of a mixture of "constantly interacting" factors. These factors include "genes, hormones, environments, [and] relationships."[2]

body produces many hormones. These are chemicals that transmit messages and regulate cell activity throughout the body. Hormones are necessary for the body to grow properly; they also affect development of the physical attributes needed for sexual reproduction. Both girls and boys have a rush of new hormones during puberty—among girls, the primary hormones include estrogen and progesterone. The changing hormone levels affect the way that girls can feel, and can make them feel anxious, moody, or even depressed.

In some teenagers personal conflicts and problems can lead to depression.

Everyone has feelings of sadness from time to time. However, when depression persists, and is accompanied by feelings of hopelessness, fatigue, and a loss of interest in life, it may be clinical depression. This is a serious mental illness that requires medical treatment.

CHAPTER THREE

What Causes Conflict?

Conflicts with others can begin when you have an emotional reaction—especially anger or fear—to something they say or do. Generally, the causes of most conflicts can be broken down into the following simple categories:

Opinions and ideas. An opinion is someone's personal judgment or view about something. Opinions are an important part of each person. They are learned from an individual's experiences and environment, and may be shaped and changed over time. You may share opinions with your parents and friends on many topics and issues. People don't always agree—whatever one person believes, there is usually someone else who believes the opposite. When people don't share the same opinions, conflicts can occur.

Opinions can also cause internal conflict. This happened to Jess. She was invited to go to the movies on Friday with Ciara, who is one of the most popular girls in her class.

Did You Know? Although you cannot prevent your emotional reaction to words or actions that make you uncomfortable, you can control how you express that reaction. The choices you make about what to do or say next can often determine whether or not a conflict results. Your words and actions can either worsen tensions or cool things down.

But she had already told her good friend Melissa that she would help her baby-sit that night. Jess wants the popular kids to like her, and she thinks that hanging out with Ciara will help. But she knows that not helping Melissa will hurt her feelings. In Jess's view that's not being a good friend. Jess has a conflict—she is torn about what to do.

Differences. All people are different—in their appearance, personality, intelligence, values and beliefs, culture, and life skills. Unfortunately, conflict often results when people focus on differences in harmful ways. They may decide to pick on the a girl who seems to stick out from the crowd, or call an overweight girl cruel names. They may reject or tease a girl because she is a different race from them, or even physically threaten her.

Being in a different environment can also cause conflict. When people are in a place that they consider familiar or safe, they feel comfortable. This sense of well-being and confidence in one's environment makes it less likely that they would engage in conflict. However, when people are in an unfamiliar place, the brain's amygdala responds to potential danger with feelings of anxiety or fear. The instinctual "fight-or-flight" response can lead a person to fight.

Possessions can be fun— or a source of conflict!

Possessions and "turf wars." From an early age, possessions are important to us. Even toddlers will fight over a toy. In American culture today, many people equate status with having things. For adults, this may mean owning a big house or a fancy sports car. For teens, it might mean having the latest designer clothes, MP3 player,

Stereotypes and Prejudice

Stereotype refers to an expectation that all members of a group are the same or will act the same way. People may form stereotypes about individuals of the same race, religion, age, looks, or culture.

Prejudice is based on stereotypes, but with an emotional factor—fear of what is different and unknown. Acts of prejudice, such as name-calling, put-downs, and violence, often occur as a result of peer pressure. One group may encourage its members to take hurtful actions against members of another group.

When you judge individuals according to their character and not their race, culture, or religion, you avoid stereotyping and prejudice. You also reduce the likelihood of conflict.

or cell phone. Whenever someone threatens to take away the things we consider our own, conflict can occur.

International conflicts—wars between two or more countries—are sometimes called "turf wars." If the government of one country feels threatened by another, or wants something that the other country possesses, it may attack. In the same way, conflict can

"It is never too late to give up our prejudices."

-Henry David Thoreau

occur when a person feels threatened by someone else. Similarly, a person who wants another's possessions may start a fight to get them. For example, if one girl is afraid that another girl will become more popular than her, she may begin teasing or harassing her rival, even if the other girl has never done anything to her.

Causes of Peer Conflict

- Rumors
- Name-calling
- Put-downs
- Boyfriend/girlfriend issues
- Threats
- Lost or damaged property

Tips for Controlling Anger

Avoid losing control. Don't let your anger or other angry people control you.

Never use your body or words to hurt others.

Get away from the situation if you think your feelings are overwhelming you.

Evaluate your choices. Think before you react!

Remember that you are responsible for your choices. No one can make you angry. That choice is up to you.[1]

CHAPTER FOUR

Resolving Conflicts

> *Cutting in front of Janelle, Carla joined her friend Letitia in the lunch line. "Thanks for holding my place," Carla told Letitia. "I really needed to talk to Mr. Z. about that report, and I didn't think it would take so long—"*
>
> *"Hey!" Janelle tapped Carla on the shoulder. "You can't cut in like that! Go to the back of the line."*
>
> *"Get your hands off me," Carla snapped. "Just mind your own business, stupid," she added, turning her back on Janelle.*

Conflicts usually become worse when the people involved do not deal with issues in healthy ways. Sarcastic comments and name-calling usually make problems worse. When people in a conflict try to resolve

Giving the silent treatment often makes conflicts worse.

their issues in respectful ways, everyone feels better.

People generally respond to conflict in one of two ways, says Ben Adkins, conflict resolution trainer and author: They either focus on the problem or they focus on the solution.[1]

If you choose the problem-focused approach, then you are constantly dwelling on what is wrong. You may try to assign blame for the problem, become defensive, or argue over the tiniest issues. You may avoid face-to-face communication, or angrily yell at the other person. Yet another strategy might be to withdraw, but complain to others. This problem-focused approach often makes conflicts worse.

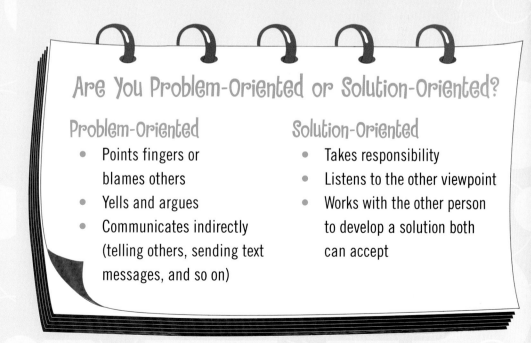

Are You Problem-Oriented or Solution-Oriented?

Problem-Oriented

- Points fingers or blames others
- Yells and argues
- Communicates indirectly (telling others, sending text messages, and so on)

Solution-Oriented

- Takes responsibility
- Listens to the other viewpoint
- Works with the other person to develop a solution both can accept

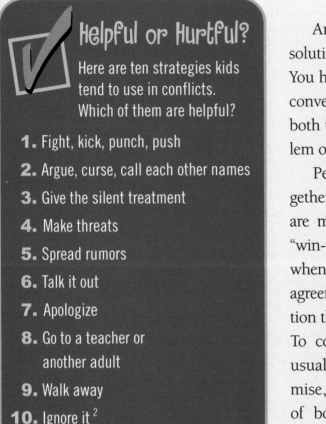

Helpful or Hurtful?

Here are ten strategies kids tend to use in conflicts. Which of them are helpful?

1. Fight, kick, punch, push
2. Argue, curse, call each other names
3. Give the silent treatment
4. Make threats
5. Spread rumors
6. Talk it out
7. Apologize
8. Go to a teacher or another adult
9. Walk away
10. Ignore it [2]

An alternative is the solution-oriented approach. You have an open, two-way conversation in which you both try to define the problem or issue.

People who work together to resolve problems are more likely to develop "win-win" solutions. That is when both sides in a disagreement develop a solution that each considers fair. To come to an agreement usually requires compromise, or a willingness of both sides to give up something in order to help resolve the conflict.

To reach a win-win solution, you have to negotiate. The word *negotiation* means reaching an agreement through discussion and compromise. For negotiation to work, you have to approach things with an open mind, and be willing to respect and listen to the other person. You can't negotiate effectively if either of you is upset or angry.

In nearly all cases, a win-win situation is the best outcome of conflict, but there are two other possible outcomes. The opposite of win-win is "lose-lose." This occurs when conflicts are resolved in such a way that both parties suffer. For example, Carla and Janelle's fight in the lunchroom got so loud that a teacher stepped in to break it up. He sent both of them to detention.

Achieving "Win-Win" Solutions

Define the problem.

What, exactly, is the conflict about? Is this fight a sign of a larger problem that one of you is having?

Talk about the problem.

Don't try to place the blame, just find out how the other person is feeling.

Think about solutions.

What are some things you can do to solve the problem? What can the other person do?

Evaluate the alternatives.

Come to an agreement on a solution that both of you can agree with.

Follow through.

Once you've agreed on the best way to handle things, stick with your decision.

A third alternative is a "win-lose" scenario. Imagine you and a friend are arguing over which movie to see—you want to see a romantic movie, and he prefers comedy films. If you give in and go see a comedy, you may be in a "win-lose" situation—he has gotten what he wants, but you haven't gotten anything you want. A lose-lose scenario would be if you couldn't agree and decided not to go to the movies at all. A win-win would occur if you could find a film that combines elements both of you like—romance and comedy. Another win-win would be if you agreed to go to his movie this time and yours next time.

CHAPTER FIVE

Don't Say "You," Say "I"

Resolving conflict by finding a win-win solution requires good communication skills. This means not only expressing how you are feeling and what is bothering you, but also listening to the other person and understanding exactly how that person feels and what is bothering him or her.

If you are upset with another girl and you feel she is at fault, your first response may be to confront her. But the way in which you speak to the person can determine whether or not the conflict can be solved easily. You may be tempted to blame the other person—after all, you're thinking, she is the one who caused the problem.

But coming right out and telling her "You were at fault because . . ." or "You were wrong because . . ." is probably going to make the situation worse, not better. This type of statement is known as a "you-message." Such a message is an attack, placing blame on the other person. Because humans instinctively defend themselves in response to attacks, a you-message is likely to make the other person argue back. It could cause a minor problem to blow up into a bigger fight.

YOU SAID YOU DID... IT'S YOUR FAULT

Using I-messages can help you avoid conversation "explosions."

You-Messages

1. "You always wait until the last minute to make plans—it's just rude!"

2. "It's not fair that you make me stay home when all of the other kids get to go to the party."

I-Messages

1. "I like doing things with you, but I prefer that you not wait until the last minute to make plans."

2. "I feel hurt that you don't trust me at my friend's party. I'd like to talk with you about this, so you can understand why it's important to me."

For example, if you are feeling annoyed because your sister "borrowed" one of your favorite sweaters without asking, you might find yourself saying something like, "You took my sweater without asking, you jerk! What were you thinking?" This you-message will most likely make your sister feel defensive. She may also get mad that you aren't treating her with respect—even though she was wrong and didn't treat you respectfully when she took your sweater without asking! Once emotions get boiling, it becomes harder to see right and wrong.

Good communication is key to relationships, and especially to resolving conflicts. While a lack of communication can lead to conflict, the way you communicate can also create problems if it makes the other person angry.

The problem with "you-messages" is that they make it seem like the person giving them is right and the other person is wrong.

Instead of placing blame, try to describe your problem in a way that does not make the other person defensive. Then explain how her action made you feel. One way to do this is by using an I-message.

An I-message typically has four parts:

1. How you feel ("*I feel* upset and annoyed…")
2. The action or incident that bothers you ("…*when* you take my things without asking…")
3. Why you feel the way you do about what happened ("…*because* I planned to wear it tonight.")
4. How you'd like the situation to be resolved ("Next time, *I want* you to ask permission first.")

Because an I-message describes only the way that you feel about a situation, people are more likely to listen to it without feeling defensive. You are letting them know there is a problem in a way that does not make them feel uncomfortable, because they are not being blamed or judged. I-messages also help the people understand you and your point of view.

When there's a conflict, I-messages can work for both sides in the dispute. For example, say your English teacher says he's feeling disappointed in you for not putting in enough work on your writing assignment. If you don't agree with his assessment, you can respond with an I-message like, "I'm surprised about this, because I spent a lot of time on the project and thought I had done what was required. I'd like a chance to

Be careful not to add blame or name-calling to an I-message.

Don't say: "I feel angry when you borrow my clothes without asking because you're such a slob I know you'll ruin them. I want you to stay out of my room."

Keep your words neutral, not hostile.

Do say: "I feel angry when you borrow my clothes without asking because they're not clean when I want to wear them. I want you to ask me next time before you borrow anything."

explain what I did." Because you are showing respect for the teacher's perspective by using an I-message, rather than a more confrontational tone, you will probably have an opportunity to discuss your side of the issue.

Although directly confronting the person you have a conflict with can be hard, it is more effective than trying to handle the situation indirectly. If you talk to everyone else—and not the person you're in conflict with—you are unlikely to bring about a resolution. If you want to change an uncomfortable situation, you need to communicate with the person causing the problem for you.

I-messages are an assertive way to confront someone. When you use them, you are being honest and direct about how you feel. You-messages, on the other hand, are aggressive,

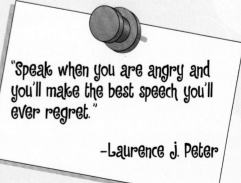

"Speak when you are angry and you'll make the best speech you'll ever regret."

–Laurence J. Peter

Quiz: How Do You Communicate?

1. Everyone in the class gets detention, even though only a few people were talking. You weren't one of them. Do you discuss the issue with your teacher after class?

    A. No, this happens all the time.
    B. Definitely. The teacher needs to know she's wrong.
    C. You plan to talk with her later in the day, after you calm down.

2. The movie ends at 10:30, but your curfew is 10:00.

    A. You decide to skip the movie and do something else.
    B. You head out to the movie anyway, knowing you'll be late getting home.
    C. You ask your parents if they'd consider giving you an exception to your regular curfew time.

3. Your boyfriend tells you Saturday afternoon that he wants to go out that night. You were looking forward to celebrating your girlfriend's birthday that night with a movie. You say:

    A. "Okay. I'm sure my girlfriend will understand that I can't make it."
    B. "What were you thinking? You know, I have a life, too."
    C. "I can't, but next weekend is good for me."

4. Two girls seem to be intentionally bumping into you in the hallway at school. The last time, you cracked your elbow on the wall and it really hurt. You say:

    A. "Oh, I'm so sorry. I didn't see you."
    B. "The next time you run into me like that, you'll be very, very sorry."
    C. "Please watch where you're going. Is there something you want to talk about?"

If your answers were mostly A's, your style is passive. Mostly B's mean an aggressive style, while C's reflect an assertive style.

Passive, Aggressive, or Assertive Communication

Your method of communication can create conflicts or make them worse. Which describes your style?

Passive—You tend to avoid saying what you really think, feel, or want. When you don't speak up for yourself or your own rights, you run the risk of being treated as a doormat by the other person.

Aggressive—You say what you think, feel, or want without respect for others' rights or feelings. Put-downs, hurtful words, and name-calling are all aggressive forms of communication that typically make the other person angry.

Assertive—You express your feelings and rights clearly, while respecting the needs and rights of others. Assertive statements in the form of I-messages are one of the most effective ways to achieve win-win conflict resolutions.

angry ways to get your point across. And if you don't speak up at all you are being passive. Using aggressive or passive forms of communication often makes conflicts worse.

The quiz shown on page 24 can help you evaluate how you deal with conflict. Is your method passive, aggressive, or assertive? Once you are aware of how you typically respond, you can take steps to change the way you communicate in order to have positive results.

CHAPTER SIX

Being a Good Listener

Clear communication is one of the most important elements of conflict resolution. But no one is a mind reader. In order to understand what another person is thinking or feeling, you have to listen to what they say. This may sound obvious, but the truth is that being a good listener can be very hard. You need to clear your head of your own thoughts and opinions. And you have to keep yourself from simply waiting for the other person to stop speaking so you can respond.

It can be especially hard to be a good listener when you're in the middle of an argument with someone. As they're listing all of the things that they are angry about, you may be mentally checking off a list of counter-charges and planning what you're going to say in response. That may help you react faster, but won't get you any closer to resolving the disagreement. In fact, it can make things worse. When you don't listen to what the other person has to say, you may appear hostile toward or critical of the person who is speaking.

Listening Checklist

An active listener:

 Is relaxed and focused on the speaker.

 Faces the speaker and looks into his or her eyes.

 Tries to feel what the speaker is feeling.

 Doesn't interrupt or get distracted.

 Lets the speaker know she's paying attention by using cues like nodding.

 Keeps an open mind.

One way to be a good listener is by using "active listening," a technique that helps you hear and clearly understand what the other person has to say. To practice active listening, choose a place to talk that is free from distractions. A bench in a quiet park is probably a better place for a conversation than a noisy table in the school lunchroom. Take turns speaking. When it's your friend's turn to speak, pay attention. Let her talk without breaking in—even if you disagree with what she's saying. This is her opportunity to talk, and you'll have a chance to respond when she's done.

As your friend speaks, look into her eyes and try to focus on what she is saying. Your goal is to be able to repeat back to

To have an effective conversation, be sure to choose a place to talk that is free from distractions.

A good listener faces the person who is talking, looks at her during the conversation, and pays close attention to what she has to say.

her the issue as she has described it. At the same time, empathize with your friend. Put yourself in her shoes, and try to understand how she feels. Show her that you are paying attention to what she is saying by nodding and saying "uh-huh" as she talks.

When your friend is finished speaking, before you address your own concerns, repeat in your own words what she has just said. The point of this is to show that you have heard and understood her side of the story.

A brief summary could go something like this: "So, it sounds like you were hurt that I didn't sit with you at lunch

What Is Empathy?

Empathy refers to the ability to understand and be sensitive to the feelings, thoughts, and experiences of another person.

today." Or give a modified I-message: "I didn't realize that you would be so upset when I didn't sit with you." If you aren't able to summarize the main issue or issues in the conflict, ask your friend to explain again, until you really do understand.

By using active listening, you can begin to understand how another person feels. However, you don't necessarily have to agree with what the other person is saying, or apologize for something that you've done. If you say something like, "You're saying that it bothers you that I asked Mark to the movies, is that right?" you are merely stating a fact about how your friend feels. You are not admitting that you did something wrong.

Active listening is important because it shows that you care for the person you're having a conflict with and are serious about wanting to resolve your disagreement. By making the other person feel like she is being listened to and understood, you increase your ability to connect with her. This can improve your chances of ending, or at least minimizing, your conflict.

"Be a good listener. Your ears will never get you in trouble."

—Frank Tyger

CHAPTER SEVEN

Mending Relationships

Maybe you started the fight, or maybe your friend did—at the moment, neither of you are speaking. You miss your friend, but you're still angry and hurt. Here are some steps you can take to reopen the lines of communication:

Make the first move. Some girls believe that if they call a friend they are fighting with, they are showing weakness or admitting that they are at fault. But the longer you wait for a friend to call the more time the anger and other emotions you're feeling can grow stronger.

When you get past your initial anger, and decide your friendship is more important than your fight, reach out to your friend. By making this first step, you're showing your friend that your friendship means a lot to you. You don't have to say you were wrong or that the argument was your fault.

When you do call, don't feel hurt if you get brushed off. While a cold response may feel like a slap in the face, your call may have surprised your friend and stirred up many confusing emotions. Chances are that by taking the first step, you will have made it easier for her to meet you halfway once she's sorted out her own feelings. Give her more time. Then try to talk again. And even if you never get the response you want—if your friend refuses to talk with you at all—

Shake on it! Being the first one to make a peace offering can save a friendship.

accept her position and move on. You'll know that you have asserted yourself and learned an important lesson about what you want and need in a friendship.

Think about what you'll say beforehand. It's good to make contact with your friend, but if you haven't thought about what you are going to say beforehand, when the conversation begins you are more likely to talk about safe topics and act like the fight never happened. That is often the easiest route to take, but the bad feelings from your conflict will not go away. If they are not addressed, the problem will flare up again sometime down the line.

It may help to write down all of the things that you want to say. That way, you can get everything out in the open right away. Otherwise, you may forget something, and later you may feel uncomfortable bringing things up again.

Girls' Top Five Conflict Starters Between Friends

- Gossip, rumors
- Having secrets told
- Boyfriends
- Feeling jealous or left out
- Mean remarks behind people's backs[1]

Conversation Openers

- "We haven't talked for a week and I miss you."
- "I want you to know how upset I am that we had a disagreement."
- "Listen, our friendship means a lot to me."

Accept responsibility, and apologize if necessary. If you caused the fight, by doing or saying something that hurt your friend's feelings, you need to take responsibility—even if your friend retaliated and did something worse to you. Apologizing for your part in a conflict will help your friend feel better. And it most likely will also help you feel better. After you take the first step by apologizing, the other person will most likely feel free to apologize in return.

Even if you believe that your friend is completely in the wrong, your apology can focus on something that you regret, such as "I'm sorry that we've gone so long without talking."[2] On the other hand, if you were at fault in the disagreement, let your friend know that you understand, that you were not trying to be mean, and that you sincerely regret the fight.

Learn to forgive. Once the fight is over, leave it in the past. When you can learn to forgive the people you fight with, you'll feel better about yourself.

Forgiveness is not something that just happens, especially when you've been hurt or humiliated. You have to make a conscious choice to forgive the other person for his or her bad behavior. Some people

"Anger makes you smaller, while forgiveness forces you to grow beyond what you were."

–Cherie Carter-Scott

Boyfriends

Different people start dating at different times, and people start serious relationships at different ages. No matter when they develop, healthy relationships share the same characteristics:

> Good communication—you can both share feelings about important things
>
> Honesty—you can trust each other
>
> Mutual respect—you can be yourself

In unhealthy relationships, conflict occurs because of negative emotions such as:

> Resentment—that your boyfriend doesn't like your friends or want you to spend any time with them
>
> Jealousy—when another girl talks to or flirts with your boyfriend
>
> Anxiety—because your boyfriend criticizes you for how you look or what you wear

believe that forgiveness lets the other person "off the hook"—that is, it lets the person out of a difficult situation. The truth is that forgiveness lets *you* off the hook. It allows you to move on with your life.

CHAPTER EIGHT

Cliques and Mean Girls

In this grade there are cliques and I hate it. Popular people diss people all the time. I know I'm part of a clique, but my clique was formed of the girls that were excluded and shunned. We like each other for who we are, and not by our hair, looks, clothes, or popularity. These girls are my real friends, no matter what happens.

—Michelle, age twelve[1]

Are there cliques in your school? Most girls your age would say yes. Cliques are informal but exclusive social groups, formed by friends or people with something in common. It can be fun to be part of a clique. Doing

It is possible to have good friends—without being cliquey.

Whispering in front of other people can make them feel left out.

things as a group can help people build really strong friendships. Unfortunately, people in cliques often torment or bully others outside their group.

The harassment is not limited to the "popular" girls putting down those who are not in their group. Even within a clique, the girls often compete for popularity. They won't fight openly. Instead, they attack each other indirectly by gossiping, backstabbing, teasing, or isolating weaker members of the clique. At the same time, they often give teachers and other adults the impression that they are being "nice" to the person they are bullying.

If you are the victim of this kind of behavior, it can be very painful—especially when you consider the teasers to be your friends or former friends. Many girls begin to doubt their own self-worth when their friends are constantly putting them down.

If you are being teased—either by someone in your clique or from outside your group of friends—a good first step is to confront the teaser. Think about what you want to say first, so

Confronting a Problem

Direct confrontation in a conflict can be a good thing. It allows you to come face-to-face with the person causing a problem for you. If you talk to everyone except the person you're in conflict with, you reduce the chances of achieving a peaceful resolution. However, if you don't feel safe about confronting the person who is harassing you, talk to an adult.

that you're prepared. You need to have a private conversation with the mean girl. Or if there is more than one, find a way to speak with each girl individually. If the person has her friends nearby, she'll feel braver and less willing to listen.

You don't have to be aggressive, but assert yourself. Use an I-message to tell the other person what has happened, how it made you feel, and what you want her to do about it: "Look, I know what you said about me. I feel really hurt that you've betrayed my trust by sharing a secret I told you, and I don't understand why you would do that. I want you to stop."

Don't let yourself get distracted if the other girl says something like, "Who told you that?" If you feel she's just stalling or trying to avoid responsibility, bring the focus back to the point you want to make: "It doesn't matter how I know—what matters is that you need to stop."

Don't hold your breath waiting for an apology. Chances are the other girl will shrug off what you've said with a laugh or a

"Whatever," and walk away. Still, you can feel good because you were able to assert yourself. You've taken a step toward resolving the conflict, and the other girl may leave you alone in the future. Your goal is not necessarily to become good friends with your tormentor—just to stop her behavior. And a good way to do that is to prove you won't be a passive victim.

If your conversation with the mean girl isn't working, the next step is to speak with a teacher or another adult authority figure about the problem. If you aren't able to talk to a teacher, ask an adult outside the school for advice. When occasional teasing becomes harassment, you may find your parents are your best supporters.

Peer Mediation

With some disagreements, it can help to ask a third person to act as a mediator. A mediator does not take sides, but listens to the complaints of both parties. By leading a discussion with the two, he or she helps them reach a compromise.

In many schools, conflicts between students are handled by peer mediators. Instead of administrators sorting out the causes of fights, students mediate problems among their classmates. Peer mediators are trained to help students solve their disagreements by listening and asking open-ended questions. They do not have the power to determine punishments. Their job is simply to help students come to their own solutions on the best ways to resolve their issues.

CHAPTER NINE

Dealing with Bullies

When Megan passed a note to Mikayla in class, Gabrielle knew the two girls were talking about her. They both looked at Gabrielle and giggled. After class, Gabrielle confronted them. "What were you writing about me?" she demanded.

Megan and Mikayla laughed. "What if we did have something to say? What are you going to do about it?" asked Mikayla.

It wasn't the first time that the two girls had teased Gabrielle. At the beginning of the school year they began to spread nasty rumors about Gabrielle. Soon, the other girls also ignored her, bumped into her in hallways, or teased her. Gabrielle felt isolated and awful.

Bullying—a pattern of harassment or violence by a stronger person against a weaker peer—is a serious problem in many schools and communities. When people speak of bullies, most think of a big boy who threatens to beat up smaller kids if they don't give him their lunch money. That type of behavior occurs mostly among boys.

However, there is another type of bullying, called relational aggression, which is more common among girls. This nonphysical form of bullying involves using relationships to harm someone else—by spreading rumors and gossip; ignoring the person; or criticizing her clothes, appearance, race, religion, or other characteristics.

Common Forms of Bullying

- Calling you names

- Making things up to get you into trouble

- Pinching, biting, or hitting

- Taking your possessions

- Encouraging your friends to exclude you from activities

- Making threats

- Making silent or abusive phone calls

- Spreading rumors about you

- Sending offensive text or instant messages, or posting insulting messages on the Internet

The victim of relational aggression may find herself being tormented at school—teased in the hallway or prevented from sitting at the lunch table. Or she may be bullied at home—while talking on her cell phone or working online at the computer. Cyberbullying occurs when someone uses e-mail, instant messaging, mobile phones, text messages, pagers, or online Web pages or posts to harass, attack, or insult another person.

There are many reasons why some girls bully others. They may believe it's what they need to do in order to hang out with

Science Says...

Studies have shown that there is a link between isolation, depression, and teen suicide. Girls who are isolated from peers are at greater risk for suicidal thoughts than girls with close friendships.[1] Nearly 5,000 teenagers commit suicide each year in the United States, making it the third-leading cause of death among teens. If you're worried that a friend is possibly suicidal (giving away possessions, avoiding friends, talking negatively about herself), share your concerns with an adult, or contact a suicide prevention hotline.

the "cool" clique. Others do it to feel better about themselves. For these girls, bullying makes them feel stronger or smarter than their victim. A few girls become bullies as a form of self-defense. They think that being mean will keep others from bullying them.

Gabrielle suffered through the torment of being bullied for several months. At school, she ate lunches alone and had no

The Surveys Say...

In 2004, KidsHealth KidsPoll surveyed more than 1,200 nine- to thirteen-year-old boys and girls about bullying. The survey found that 86 percent had seen someone else being bullied. Almost half—48 percent—said they were victims of bullies, while 42 percent admitted that they sometimes bullied other kids.[2]

What Can You Do If You Are Being Bullied?

- Tell an adult.

- Tell the bully to stop; then calmly walk away.

- Do not fight back because you could also end up in trouble.

- Lighten the mood and distract people by making a joke.

- Make new friends and get involved in activities that interest you.

- Don't blame yourself.

- Be strong and believe in yourself—it's the bully who has a problem, not you.[3]

one to talk to. At night, she would cry in her room after finishing her homework. She tried talking to the girls, but it did not help. Eventually, she spoke to the principal. After he ordered the girls to disband their anti-Gabrielle "club," things got a little better, but Gabrielle still felt isolated for the rest of the year.

Isolation can be incredibly painful. In addition to feeling anger and frustration, the person who is isolated may feel bewildered about why someone would want to torture them. They may also feel ashamed about themselves, believing that some flaw in their character meant they deserved to be bullied. That attitude is wrong, but without support, it is hard for victims of bullying to overcome such feelings. The hurt caused by bullying can last for years.

Have You Been Bullied Online?

If you can answer yes to any of the following questions, then you have been the victim of cyberbullying:

1. Have you had personal information about yourself posted online without your consent?

2. Has a private conversation between you and a friend ever been posted without your knowledge or permission?

3. Have you had an embarrassing picture of yourself posted online without your knowledge or permission?

4. Have you been entered into a Web site survey or contest without your consent?

5. Has anyone pretended to be you online?

Six Ways to Avoid Online Bullies

1. Don't give out private information, especially passwords.

2. Don't exchange pictures or give out e-mail addresses to people you meet on the Internet.

3. Don't send a message when you are angry—it's hard to undo things that are said in anger.

4. Don't open or read messages from people you don't know.

5. Recognize that online conversations can be copied, printed, and shared. They're not private.

6. Use blocking features to keep bullies from bothering you during chat or instant messaging sessions.[4]

If you are being bullied, don't just keep it to yourself and hope the problem will go away. Confront the bully and ask her or him to stop, if you feel safe doing that. Psychologist Sharon Lamb suggests that the victim of a bully handle confrontation with dignity, using words to express her feelings and stand up for herself.[6] While confronting the bully, she should try to stay calm. Bullies typically want to see a victim embarrass herself by dissolving into tears or yelling in anger. When the response is cool, they'll often move on to someone else.

Suppose you're not the victim of relational aggression, but know someone else who is. You have the power to stop a bully. If you see someone being teased, you can tell the bully that you don't find her dramatics very funny. If you don't feel comfortable about speaking up, then simply walk away. Don't give the bully an audience. Similarly, don't participate in the spreading of rumors, signing of secret petitions, or online gossiping. Your refusal to go along with the crowd can be an example that could help others do the same. That might be enough to end the bully's cruel behavior. Whether you are a victim or spectator, if the abuse doesn't stop, you need to tell an adult.

CHAPTER TEN

"My Parents Don't Understand Me!"

Maria was excited. Alisha had invited her to come by her home after school so they could work together on a group science project. Maria's family had just moved into the neighborhood, and Maria was new to the middle school. She was looking forward to the chance to hang out with Alisha.

However, after dropping off her backpack at home, Maria found out that her mother expected her to clean up her room first. "But Mom," Maria protested. "I told Alisha I'd be there by 3:30. I'll get the work done tonight."

"You're just going to have to tell this girl that you'll be there after you finish your chores," her mother responded.

Maria burst into tears. "You just don't get it, do you?" she yelled at her mother as she stormed out the door. "I'll come home when I'm good and ready!"

Conflicts between parents and their teenage children are quite common. When you were young, you depended on your parents for everything. But during the teen years, you are starting to want to make your own decisions about your clothes, friends, after-school activities, dating, and other things. All teens feel this natural drive to become more independent. However, differences between what you want (to be independent) and what parents want (to protect and guide you) can often lead to fights. In most families, these arguments become rare over time, as parents accept that their teenage children are capable of making good decisions.

Maria has found herself fighting constantly with her mother lately. She says she's tired of her mother always telling her what she can and can't do. Maria wants more freedom, especially since she needs to make new friends. However, her mother is not ready to grant Maria that independence.

The desire for independence isn't the only issue that can come between kids and their parents. When report card grades don't meet parents' expectations, most teens figure they're in trouble with their mom and dad. But teens can also have conflicts when their opinions about what is important differ from those of their mother or father. Kids often complain that their parents don't understand their problems, or don't treat them fairly. For example, sometimes parents step in to stop fights between brothers and sisters—and then don't give one sibling the chance to tell his or her side of the story.

You may think that your parents don't understand you. But, if you want your parents to understand you, you have to help them out. Explain your needs and feelings—why going to a particular party or wearing a certain outfit is important to you, for example. You don't have to tell

Common Conflict Starters at Home

- Sharing possessions
- Fights with siblings
- Report card grades
- Room privacy
- Chores

Chores may not be fun—but they need to be done!

How Do You Relate to Your Parents?

What do you think your parents really mean when they ask you questions like these?

"Where are you going tonight?"

A. Is it a safe place?

B. We need to know where you are at all times!

C. We are sure it is bad.

"Who will you be with?"

A. Can we trust them with your safety?

B. We don't trust your friends.

C. Are they wild?

"We want you home by 11:00 P.M.!"

A. We need our sleep—and like it or not, we don't rest well until we know you are safe.

B. You can't be trusted to be out any later.

C. Kids always get into trouble after then.

"Don't talk back to me!"

A. I deserve more respect than that.

B. It is rude and I did not raise a rude child.

C. What I say goes, like it or not!

If most of your answers were:

A's, you believe your parents respect you but set rules for your safety.

B's, you believe your parents don't trust you and are more concerned about what the neighbors think than about what you think.

C's, you believe your parents always think the worst of you.

If your answers were mostly **B**'s and **C**'s, it's time to sit down and have a talk with your parents. You probably need to make some changes in how you treat each other.[1]

them everything. After all, everyone needs some privacy. But you should be open about major things that are going on in your life.

Disagreements with parents are inevitable, but it won't help if you blow up every time you are angry. If you feel the urge to yell and scream because your parents won't let you hang out with friends—leave the room. Give yourself some time to cool down and think about the best way to approach your conflict.

For example, Maria could have gone to her bedroom until she calmed down. Then, she could have had a conversation with her mother to explain her point of view. Some of the I-messages Maria could have used include: "I understand that you want me to be responsible about my chores, but I was planning to get them done tonight. I am upset because I need

Conflicts will happen. But being respectful toward your parents can help prevent big fights.

Tips on Talking to Parents and Other Adults

Bring up your issue when the adult has the time to listen. Don't try to talk to your parents when they're busy with something or someone else or rushing out the door. Say, "Is this a good time for you? I have something important to discuss."

Be aware of your body language. Don't roll your eyes, cross your arms, or clench your fists. Look the other person in the eyes and try to remain calm.

Use respectful language. Don't use sarcasm, insults, or put-downs when explaining your point of view. Snapping something like, "That's a stupid reason," will only make the other person angrier.

Be honest. Tell the truth about how you feel or what has happened; your parents and other adults want to trust you.

Listen to the other side of the issue. The adult will be more likely to show you the same respect.

State your case using "I-messages." "I feel pressured because I need to get this report done tonight so I don't really have time walk the dog," or "I don't agree because . . . ."

to get my schoolwork done, and Alisha is counting on me to be there."

While you are talking, be calm but assertive. After explaining to your parents why an issue is important to you, ask them—respectfully—if they'd be willing to change their minds. You could offer to do something in return, to show that you deserve greater responsibility. For example, Maria could offer to babysit her little brother on weekday evenings in exchange for free time right after school.

Your parents may still say "no"—and if so, you'll have to abide by their rules. But they'll appreciate your approach. Showing your parents that you can deal with disagreements calmly and rationally may help you in the long run. When you show that you can be responsible, your parents will be more likely to give you greater freedom. If you can handle that, a major source of family conflict will be gone.

Conflicts with Other Adults

Parents are not the only adults you may find yourself in conflict with. All teens need to learn how to deal with conflicts involving teachers, counselors, neighbors, store clerks, and others. The key to avoiding or resolving these conflicts is to treat adults with respect, while still asserting your own rights or opinions.

If you believe your teacher has unfairly given you a bad grade, for example, don't stand up in front of the class and accuse her of hating you. Doing that shows a lack of respect for the teacher. She won't take your complaint seriously, and you'll probably be sent to the principal's office. Instead, restrain your anger. At the end of class ask the teacher if she will meet with you privately after school to talk about the grade. Before that meeting, think about the reasons why you feel the grade is unfair—it may help to write them down. That way, you're prepared when you speak to the teacher.

CHAPTER ELEVEN

Sibling Rivalry

Conflicts between siblings, or sibling rivalry, **occur in every family.** Few brothers and sisters are born with the natural ability to share and work out their differences. So it is natural that fighting occurs from time to time.

Perhaps the most common emotion, and the main reason brothers and sisters fight, is jealousy. If you find yourself saying things like "My sister is prettier than I am" or "My parents only pay attention to my brother," you're going to feel pretty lousy. Those feelings can show themselves through other emotions, like anger ("My brother is always taking my things"), resentment ("It annoys me that my little brother gets all the attention"), and guilt ("I feel bad that I'm mean to my sister").

If you're upset with your siblings, don't try to "punish" them by ignoring them or being nasty. Instead, try using I-messages to talk with them. Then, listen to their side. Ask your sister what is bothering her. Listen to your brother's explanation. Get things out in the open.

If you're jealous because you think your parents are favoring your brother or sister, don't let that feeling grow stronger. If your sister gets a gift but you didn't, ask yourself if your parents had a special reason to reward her. Be honest:

Birth Order

Studies have shown that the order in which children are born affects the way they interact in the family. In many families the oldest child is given the most responsibility, while the youngest child is often treated as the "baby." Here are some birth order characteristics:

Oldest child: high achiever, leader, prone to stress, reliable, follows rules.

Middle child: learns to give and take, peacemaker, sometimes feels unloved, avoids conflict.

Youngest child: show-off who loves attention, likes people, most spoiled.

Only child: mature, shy in groups, articulate, somewhat self-centered.[1]

In similar circumstances, have they done nice things for you that they haven't done for your sister? If so, there's no reason for you to be jealous. If not, you need to ask your parents if you can talk. The conversation will make them aware of how their actions have affected you, and you'll feel better, too, when you share your feelings.

"I-Messages"

- "I feel angry when you go in my room and mess with my stuff."
- "I don't want you in my room unless you ask me first."

CHAPTER TWELVE

Divorce and Blended Families

After her father remarried, Sarah found that she and her new stepmother didn't agree on many things. Sarah resented being grounded for behavior that had never bothered her mother.

To make matters worse, Sarah's mother and stepmother do not get along, so at Sarah's dance recitals, the two families sit apart. Sarah thinks her stepmom is cold and standoffish. "We just don't talk," Sarah explains.

Changing family situations can trigger a range of feelings for all involved.

I**t's normal for kids to feel a range of emotions when parents divorce.** You may feel angry, hurt, guilty, and sad. You may also feel fearful about the future, because your living situation is likely to change. If your parents have involved you in their tensions with each other, you may feel glad to no longer feel caught in between them. And you may worry that your parents will remarry. Then you will have to learn how to deal with new relationships.

There are more than 22 million stepfamilies in the United States, and it is estimated that about 1,300 new ones form each day, on average.[1] These blended families are established when an adult who has children remarries. For example, if a divorced woman with custody of her two children marries a widowed man

Tips for Coping with the Stress of Divorce

- Bring your concerns out in the open at the earliest possible time.

- If your parents are angry with each other, ask them not to make you take sides.

- Make it clear that you want your parents to work out their differences so that they will both attend events that are important to you, such as games, plays, or recitals.

- Write down your feelings in a journal.

- Talk about your feelings with your siblings (they may need more support than you do), a friend, or another adult.

who is raising a daughter, the children will be considered stepchildren of both parents.

When a blended family is created, children worry about many things. A girl may wonder if the new stepfather is being

Did You Know? A blended family is formed when adults who already have children marry.

Tips for Getting Along with a Stepparent

- Try doing nice things to include your stepparent in the family: say thanks for a lift or a meal; acknowledge him or her with a friendly hello in the morning and when you come home.

- Extend invitations to your sports events or school functions.

- Treat him or her as you would like to be treated—with respect.[2]

nice to her just because he married her mother, or if he really likes her as a person. She may fear that she is not really part of the family, or suspect that her stepsiblings don't really like her. She may worry about getting along with her new family or about living in a new place. Often, a teen in a blended family may wish that things would go back to the way they used to be. But that is not going to happen.

With so many new fears, anxieties, and other emotions involved, members of blended families often find it hard to avoid conflict. In fact, according to statistics cited in an article in *Psychology Today*, 60 percent of remarriages end in divorce.[3] But with time and effort, stepfamily members can become close and loving. "Experts say it typically takes four to eight years for a new family to blend—to feel like a real family rather than a stepfamily," says author Jim Killam in an article about the troubles faced by blended families.[4]

Often, there is a period of adjustment before stepparents and their children can work things out. Sometimes, however, conflicts arise on a daily basis, and the family members have to find a way to deal with them.

Conflicts can occur not only between stepparents and children but also between stepsiblings. For example, fourteen-year-old Madison and her eighteen-year-old stepbrother John had a problem that was causing them to fight. Someone had to get up early on the weekends to take the family dog for a walk, but both of them wanted to sleep in. They negotiated a verbal agreement to take turns: Madison would get up early on Saturdays, letting John sleep late. And Madison could sleep late on Sundays, while John walked the dog.

This is an example of a "win-win" arrangement, because both stepsiblings were getting something that they wanted. As with all conflicts, respect and an understanding of the other person's needs makes it easier to eliminate disagreements.

The bottom line is, when you're in a blended family everyone will have to work harder to get along. Even if you love and care for the new members of your family, there are going to be times when they get on your nerves or make you angry. When you begin to get annoyed, remind yourself that no family is perfect. Try not to always find fault with them— or with yourself.

"The most important trip you may take in life is meeting people half way."

-Henry Boyle

Treat your parents and stepparents the same way you want to be treated.

Everyone Feels This Way

Remember, you are not the only person who feels anger, frustration, guilt, shame, or anxiety about conflicts in your life. Everyone experiences conflict. Learning to deal with disagreements is an essential part of growing up. The knowledge you gain each time you deal with a conflict will help you in the future, when you encounter new issues.

The teen years are hard for everyone. Look around—all of your classmates, both boys and girls, are feeling many of the same inner conflicts that you are. The choices you make regarding how you will approach and deal with conflict will shape the person you become.

The best way to resolve conflicts is through assertive communication. Stand up for yourself and for what you believe in. This doesn't mean that you should always insist on having your own way—that's bullying. Instead, always try to understand the other person's perspective. Then, try to work together to find a win-win solution.

Did You Know?

The term self-esteem refers to the way you feel about yourself. If your self-esteem is low, you are unhappy or annoyed with yourself, or don't think your life is valuable. On the other hand, if you recognize that people love you for who you are, and value your opinions, beliefs, and values, you have high self-esteem.

When you are respectful, understanding, and assertive, you can work out conflicts.

Sometimes, you will find it hard to assert yourself. And sometimes you won't succeed in resolving a conflict to your satisfaction. That's normal, and it's okay. Don't beat yourself up about it, but don't forget how bad you felt. Get a little angry, and allow that emotion to give you courage to stand up for yourself the next time. In the long run, learning how to be assertive will help you feel good about yourself.

Many teens try to hide their anxieties and insecurities behind a mask of self-confidence. While it's good to express confidence in yourself, it's also okay to admit when you're feeling scared, angry, happy, or ashamed. It's better to be honest about your feelings and emotions. That way, you will feel better about yourself as a person.

Don't hide behind "masks" of your emotions— be honest and tell others how you feel.

Everyone Feels This Way

Chapter 1. Conflict and Your Emotions

1. Carroll E. Izard, *The Psychology of Emotions* (New York: Plenum Press, 1991), p. 244.

2. Ibid.

3. Ibid.

Chapter 2. Your Brain Under Confict

1. Louann Brizendine, *The Female Brain* (New York: Morgan Road Books, 2006).

2. Robin Marantz Henig, "How Women Think," *New York Times*, September 10, 2006.

3. Adapted from *Family First Aid Help for Troubled Teens*, "Teen Depression Statistics and Warning Signs," n.d., <http://www.familyfirstaid.org/depression.html> (March 27, 2007).

Chapter 3. What Causes Conflict?

1. Adapted from U.S. Centers for Disease Control and Prevention, "Bam! Guide to Getting Along," *BAM Body and Mind*, n.d., <http://www.bam.gov/sub_yourlife/yourlife_conflict_3.html> (March 27, 2007).

Chapter 4. Resolving Conflicts

1. Ben Adkins, "Adjust Your Point of View in Order to Resolve Conflict," *Fort Worth Business Press*, February 27–March 5, 2000, p. 43.

2. Naomi Drew, *The Kids Guide to Working Out Conflicts: How to Keep Cool, Stay Safe, and Get Along* (Minneapolis, Minn.: Free Spirit Publishing, 2004), p. 14.

Chapter 7. Mending Relationships

1. Drew, p. 7.

2. Ellen Welty, "How to Make up with a Friend," *Redbook*, December 2005, p. 113.

Chapter 8. Cliques and Mean Girls

1. Rosalind Wiseman, *Queen Bees and Wannabes: Helping Your Daughter Survive Cliques, Gossip, Boyfriends, and Other Realities of Adolescence* (New York: Three Rivers Press, 2002), p. 22.

Chapter 9. Dealing with Bullies

1. David Williamson, "Research Reveals Social Isolation Boosts Teen Girls' Suicide Thoughts," *University of North Carolina News Services*, January 5, 2004, <http://www.unc.edu/news/archives/jan04/bear010504.html> (March 27, 2007).

2. Nemours Foundation, "Kids Health: Bullying and Your Child," n.d., <http://www.kidshealth.org/parent/emotions/behavior/bullies.html> (March 27, 2007).

3. From "Bring Bullying to an End," *GirlsHealth.gov Fact Sheet,* n.d., <http://www.4girls.gov/factsheets/bullying.pdf> (March 27, 2007).

4. Adapted from i-Safe America, "Beware of the Cyber Bully," n.d., <http://www.isafe.org/imgs/pdf/education/CyberBullying.pdf> (March 27, 2007).

5. Adapted from i-Safe America, "Cyber Bullying: Statistics and Tips," n.d., <http://www.isafe.org/channels/sub.php?ch=op&sub_id=media_cyber_bullying> (March 27, 2007).

6. Quoted in Nanci Hellmich, "Caught in the Catty Corner," *USA Today*, April 9, 2002, p. D–1.

Chapter 10. "My Parents Don't Understand Me!"

1. Adapted from *About: Teen Advice*, "Quiz: Parent Speak, Are You Fluent?" n.d., <http://teenadvice.about.com/library/teenquiz/35/blparentspeakquiz.htm> (March 27, 2007).

Chapter 11. Sibling Rivalry

1. Adapted from Kevin Leman, *The New Birth Order Book: Why You Are the Way You Are* (New York: Revell, 1998), p. 33.

Chapter 12. Divorce and Blended Families

1. Bao Ong, "Family: New Ties? New Stuff!" *Newsweek*, July 18, 2005.

2. Adapted from Children, Youth, and Women's Health Service, "Step-families," November 8, 2005, <http://www.cyh.com/HealthTopics/HealthTopicDetails.aspx?p=243&np=291&id=2382> (March 27, 2007).

3. Hara Estroff Marano, "Divorced?—Remarriage in America," *Psychology Today*, March 2000.

4. Jim Killam, "Dangerous Crossing," *Marriage Partnership*, Spring 2004, p. 46.

active listening—A technique in which the listener focuses intently on hearing and understanding what another person is saying.

amygdala—A part of the brain that regulates emotions.

anxiety—Feelings of fear, apprehension, and worry.

clique—A small, exclusive group of people, usually held together by common interests or views.

compromise—An agreement in which both sides agree to give up something in order to resolve a conflict.

conflict—A struggle that results from disagreements about needs, wishes, demands, or opinions.

consequence—The result of an action.

depression—Long-lasting feelings of sadness and hopelessness and a loss of interest in life.

emotion—A strong reaction to an outside event. Some emotions include anger, frustration, joy, grief, and shame.

empathy—The ability to understand another person's feelings, thoughts, and experiences.

hormone—A chemical substance that signals body cells to action.

I-messages—Solution-oriented statements using the word "I" rather than "you" and expressing the speaker's feelings in a non-threatening way.

mediator—A person who doesn't take sides in a conflict, but helps bring about resolution by helping the opposing parties communicate and figure out an agreement.

negotiate—To come to an agreement through discussion and compromise.

puberty—The developmental stage in which the human body is maturing to adulthood.

relational aggression—A nonphysical form of bullying using relationships to harm someone else.

self-esteem—The level of confidence and satisfaction a person feels about himself or herself.

FURTHER READING

Canfield, Jack, et al. *Chicken Soup for the Girl's Soul: Real Stories by Real Girls About Real Stuff.* Deerfield Beach, Fla.: Health Communications, 2005.

Drew, Naomi. *The Kids' Guide to Working Out Conflicts: How to Keep Cool, Stay Safe, and Get Along.* Minneapolis, Minn.: Free Spirit Publishing, 2004.

Judson, Karen. *Resolving Conflicts: How to Get Along When You Don't Get Along.* Berkeley Heights, N.J.: Enslow Publishers, Inc., 2005.

INTERNET ADDRESSES

Kids Health: Dealing with Feelings

http://www.kidshealth.org/kid/feeling/

Relationships: Dealing With Conflict

http://www.girlshealth.gov/relationships/
conflict_resolution.htm

Stop Bullying Now!

http://stopbullyingnow.hrsa.gov/index.asp?area=main

HOTLINE TELEPHONE NUMBERS

National Domestic Violence Hotline

1-800-799-SAFE (1-800-799-7233)

National Suicide Prevention Lifeline

1-800-273-TALK (1-800-273-8255)

CONTRIBUTORS

Author **Dorothy Kavanaugh** is a freelance writer who lives near Philadelphia. She holds a bachelor's degree in elementary education from Bryn Mawr College. She has written many nonfiction titles for young adults.

Series advisor **Dr. Carroll Izard** is the Trustees Distinguished Professor of Psychology at the University of Delaware. His research and writing focuses on the development of emotion knowledge and emotion regulation and their contributions to social and emotional competence. He is author or editor of seventeen books (one of which won a national award) and more than one hundred articles in scientific journals. Dr. Izard is a fellow of both national psychological associations and the American Association for the Advancement of Science. He is the winner of the American Psychological Association's G. Stanley Hall Award and an international exchange fellowship from the National Academy of Sciences.

A Guys' Guide to Anger; A Girls' Guide to Anger
ISBN-13: 978-0-7660-2853-1   ISBN-10: 0-7660-2853-4

A Guys' Guide to Conflict; A Girls' Guide to Conflict
ISBN-13: 978-0-7660-2852-4   ISBN-10: 0-7660-2852-6

A Guys' Guide to Jealousy; A Girls' Guide to Jealousy
ISBN-13: 978-0-7660-2854-8   ISBN-10: 0-7660-2854-2

A Guys' Guide to Loneliness; A Girls' Guide to Loneliness
ISBN-13: 978-0-7660-2856-2   ISBN-10: 0-7660-2856-9

A Guys' Guide to Love; A Girls' Guide to Love
ISBN-13: 978-0-7660-2855-5   ISBN-10: 0-7660-2855-0

A Guys' Guide to Stress; A Girls' Guide to Stress
ISBN-13: 978-0-7660-2857-9   ISBN-10: 0-7660-2857-7

{FLIP-iT-OVER}
GUIDES TO TEEN EMOTIONS

A Guys' Guide to

Conflict

Jim Gallagher

E **Enslow Publishers, Inc.**
40 Industrial Road
Box 398
Berkeley Heights, NJ 07922
USA

http://www.enslow.com

Library of Congress Cataloging-in-Publication Data

    Gallagher, Jim, 1969- A guys' guide to conflict ; A girls' guide to conflict / Jim Gallagher and Dorothy Cavenaugh.
      p. cm. — (Flip-it-over guides to teen emotions)
     No collective t.p.; titles transcribed from individual title pages.
     Includes bibliographical references and index.
     ISBN-13: 978-0-7660-2852-4
     ISBN-10: 0-7660-2852-6
     1. Conflict management—Juvenile literature. 2. Boys—Life skills guides—Juvenile literature.
    3. Girls—Life skills guides—Juvenile literature. I. Gallagher, Jim, 1969- Guy's guide to conflict.
    II. Title. III. Title: Guys' guide to conflict.

    HM1126.C38 2008
    303.6'9—dc22

                   2007026457

Printed in the United States of America.

10 9 8 7 6 5 4 3 2 1

Produced by OTTN Publishing, Stockton, NJ.

To Our Readers: We have done our best to make sure all Internet Addresses in this book were active and appropriate when we went to press. However, the author and the publisher have no control over and assume no liability for the material available on those Internet sites or on other Web sites they may link to. Any comments or suggestions can be sent by e-mail to comments@enslow.com or to the address on the title page.

Photo Credits: © Bonnie Kamin/PhotoEdit, p. 56; © Cindy Charles/PhotoEdit, p. 39; © David Young-Wolff/PhotoEdit, p. 50; Illustration by JimHunt.us, pp. 9, 10, 47; ImageState, p. 32; © iStockphoto.com/Dawna Stafford, p. 52; © iStockphoto.com/Jani Bryson, p. 54; © iStockphoto.com/Jim Kolaczko, p. 6; © iStockphoto.com/Timothy Robbins, p. 36; © 2007 Jupiterimages Corporation, pp. 3, 4, 16, 25, 26, 42, 57; © Michael Newman/PhotoEdit, pp. 1, 28; Used Under License from Shutterstock, Inc., pp. 18, 20, 30, 34, 46.

Cover Photo: © Michael Newman/PhotoEdit

CONTENTS

What Is Conflict?

> All of the students in Mr. Ziff's tenth-grade English class are working on a group project related to the play Romeo and Juliet. The members of one group—Marco, Dan, Donald, and Melissa—cannot agree on how to do the assignment. Marco wants the group to rewrite a scene from the play so that it is set in modern times, and then act it out in class. However, Dan and Donald would prefer to write a report they can hand in. Melissa doesn't really like either idea.

Marco, Dan, Donald, and Melissa have a conflict. A conflict is what happens when there is a disagreement over two or more ideas, needs, desires, feelings, or expectations. In this case, the four students must figure out how they can work out their differences and do a good job on their project.

Everyone experiences conflict at one time or another. It is a normal part of life. But conflicts can become problems when they are not resolved in healthy ways. If people do not discuss and work out their differences, they can become tense, angry,

Like a game of tug-of-war, conflict involves opponents striving to be in control.

and frustrated. In some cases conflicts can even lead to violence.

> "The greatest conflicts are not between two people but between one person and himself."
>
> —Garth Brooks

When you are in your early teens—a time when you are experiencing a jumble of emotions and powerful new feelings—conflict can be very difficult to manage. Sometimes young people can feel so overwhelmed by pressure that they make some bad choices. For example, they try to escape from their problems by engaging in dangerous or harmful behaviors, such as drug or alcohol abuse. Some even have thoughts of suicide.

The good news is that you can learn the skills to manage or resolve conflicts in a healthy way. Learning how to handle conflict takes practice and training, but the skills involved are important and can be used throughout your life.

Conflicts Can Occur...

- in your personal relationships: with family, friends, and teachers
- in society: among people with different values or religions, or from different ethnic groups
- within yourself: when you have to make a hard decision or you learn something different from your previous beliefs

How Conflict Makes You Feel

> During a soccer game, Jeff's shot on goal smashed right into Carlos's face. As Carlos staggered back, Jeff let out a laugh. "What's so funny?" Carlos snapped. "That hurt!"
>
> "What? Can't you take it?" snorted Jeff, as he scooped up the ball.
>
> His heart pounding, Carlos glared at his opponent. His face was bright red—both from the impact of the ball and from anger. His hands tensed into fists.

Perhaps the reason that most people think of conflict in negative terms is because it can be a very unpleasant experience. When a disagreement starts, you suddenly experience a rush of strong feelings—your emotions. The most common emotion associated with conflict is anger. However, other feelings may include disgust, contempt, fear, anxiety, shame, guilt, and sadness.

Anger is a powerful emotion that can have a wide range of intensities. You might say that you are angry when you are merely

In whatever sport you play, try to keep your cool when things go wrong.

Anger can be directed outward (when you feel angry at someone else) or inward (when you feel angry with yourself).

irritated about something. But you use the same word to describe being furious and in a rage. Disgust and contempt are two emotions that often accompany feelings of anger. Disgust refers to feelings of horrified distaste for something or someone. Contempt is a feeling that someone is inferior or does not deserve respect.

If you are in a conflict that lasts for a long period of time, you may also experience emotions of fear and anxiety over real or imagined danger. For example, worry and fear resulting from being teased and bullied at school can make

Science Says...

When you feel certain emotions, the body often responds in specific ways.

Anger and fear: increased heartbeat and an involuntary tensing of muscles

Shame: facial blushing and warmth in the upper chest or face

Sadness: tears, tightness in the throat, and heaviness in the limbs

some people become physically ill with intense headaches and overpowering nausea.

Two other emotions, shame and guilt, are also linked to conflicts, although they are rarely present during the heat of an argument. If you lose your cool during a disagreement, you may feel embarrassed afterward. This is especially true if people you like and respect witnessed your angry outburst. You may also feel guilty about having hurt a friend verbally or physically during a fight. These feelings can lead to feeling another powerful emotion—sadness—for your role in the conflict.

The mixture of emotions that accompany conflict can have a physical impact. Obviously, if you get into an argument that

You and Your Emotions

A part of everyone's personality, emotions are a powerful driving force in life. They are hard to define and understand. But what is known is that emotions—which include anger, fear, love, joy, jealousy, and hate—are a normal part of the human system. They are responses to situations and events that trigger bodily changes, motivating you to take some kind of action.

Some studies show that the brain relies more on emotions than on intellect in learning and in making decisions. Being able to identify and understand the emotions in yourself and in others can help you in your relationships with family, friends, and others throughout your life.

Science Says...

When you become angry, your body responds by feeling strong and ready for action. As a result, you are more capable of physically defending yourself. "Anger prepares us for action," explains psychology researcher Carroll E. Izard. "It bolsters physical strength and courage to match the impulse to act. We may never feel stronger or more invigorated than when we are really angry."[1] Many sociologists believe that the emotion of anger played an important role in the survival of the earliest human beings. Anger made these humans stronger and able to confront dangerous threats, such as wild animals or other enemies.

turns into a fistfight, you can get hurt. But conflicts that do not involve punching or other violence can cause physical changes in the body. After an unpleasant disagreement, you might feel exhausted or weak afterward. Conflict causes some teens to get headaches or stomachaches, and others to feel dizzy or lightheaded. Other symptoms related to problems with conflict are having trouble sleeping, difficulty concentrating, and worrying.

"If you are patient in one moment of anger, you will escape a hundred days of sorrow."

—Ancient Chinese Proverb

Finding Solutions

Recently, fifteen-year-old Cody has been fighting a lot with his parents. Cody's parents have been giving him a hard time about his clothes—he always wears a black shirt, jeans, and jacket. They criticize his hair, which is long and shaggy and often covers his eyes. Cody's parents complain that he and his friends seem to spend all of their time on their skateboards.

Cody is a B student and has never been in trouble at school or with the law. He doesn't understand why his parents need to say anything about how he dresses, or how he spends his time.

Although all conflicts are different, they share three basic elements—issues, strategies, and outcomes. Issues are the reasons that a conflict occurs. For example, one issue causing problems between Cody and his parents is his desire to be seen as an individual, while his parents wish their son were more clean-cut.

Many different kinds of issues cause conflict. People who feel threatened may want to protect themselves, their possessions, or things they respect. Conflict can occur when people hold opinions and beliefs that differ with those of others. People who believe very strongly in something generally feel that those who disagree with them are wrong.

Disagreements over how kids should dress are a common issue with parents.

Good and Not-So-Good Strategies Teens Use in Conflicts

1. Fight, kick, punch, push
2. Argue, curse, call each other names
3. Give the silent treatment
4. Make threats
5. Spread rumors
6. Talk it out
7. Apologize
8. Go to a teacher or another adult
9. Walk away
10. Ignore it[1]

Sometimes, conflict occurs just because someone looks or acts differently from others in the neighborhood. Strangers who wear unusual clothes or speak with a foreign accent may be viewed with alarm. Conflicts can occur because of ethnic, racial, or religious differences as well.

The ways that people react to and deal with conflict are called strategies. Some strategies used by teens might include fighting, talking over problems, or telling an adult.

The third element of a conflict is its result, or outcome. It is determined by the strategies a person uses to resolve the

problem. With every conflict, there are four possible outcomes:[2]

1. **No solution.** Sometimes, the issue will simply be dropped. Cody's parents may stop hassling him about his appearance, for example. However, nothing is solved. And there is no guarantee that the issue will not arise again.

2. **Giving in.** Cody could give in and do what his parents want. By submitting to their wishes, he is making a conscious decision to let go of the argument. He may think, "Right now, my parents make the rules. To avoid conflict, I'll obey them. After all, I'll be on my own soon." By giving in to his parents' wishes to make them happy, Cody is giving his parents a high level of control over his life. And he most likely feels frustrated. This frustration may grow into feelings of resentment and anger that would make future conflicts with his parents more likely.

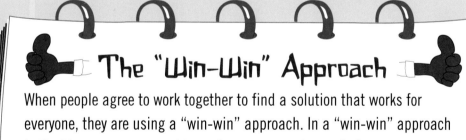

The "Win-Win" Approach

When people agree to work together to find a solution that works for everyone, they are using a "win-win" approach. In a "win-win" approach both sides are encouraged to work as partners instead of opponents. Instead of each side attacking the other to try to gain an advantage, they try to come up with a solution that is fair to both parties. Compromise, bargaining, and seeking alternatives are the key components to achieving a "win-win" outcome.

3. **An adult-imposed solution.** This outcome is essentially the same as giving in, but it occurs because Cody's parents have forced their son to obey their wishes. As with the giving in outcome, Cody's resentment over being forced to change would make the situation unpleasant for everyone.

4. **A solution acceptable to both sides.** Both Cody and his parents would have to discuss the issue and agree on a compromise solution that each can be happy with. This outcome has the best chance of long-term success. If both parties believe they are getting something they want from the solution, both will be able to support it.

Of the four possible outcomes to conflict, a solution that is acceptable to both sides is usually best. However, it can also be the most difficult one to achieve. To reach an agreement, all parties involved in the conflict must treat others with respect and work together to understand the problem and determine a solution.

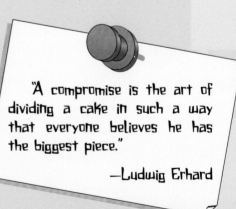

"A compromise is the art of dividing a cake in such a way that everyone believes he has the biggest piece."

—Ludwig Erhard

CHAPTER FOUR

Effective Communication

> "You can have my science book. I'll see if I can get another copy."
>
> "You idiot! What are doing? That's my book! Give it back!"
>
> "I don't like it that you took my science book without asking, but we can share during class until you replace your old one."

hese three responses to a potential conflict reflect the three main styles of communication: passive, aggressive, and assertive. Depending on how you deal with a conflict, you may make use all three of these styles.

People who are passive communicators try to avoid conflict with others by giving in to them. They may say things like "I don't know" or "Whatever you think is fine." Passive communicators may be afraid of making someone else uncomfortable or unhappy. However, by always putting others' needs ahead of their own, they invite others to take advantage of them. While they may head off a conflict, they may feel unhappy because their needs are not being met.

By contrast, aggressive communicators always "look out for number one." They seem to believe that others are not as important as they are. They may intentionally take

> "The strong man is the man who can stand up for his rights and not hit back."
>
> —Dr. Martin Luther King, Jr.

advantage of, hurt, humiliate, or put down others. The aggressive communicator says things like, "Can't you see that my way is best?" or "Your idea is stupid and will never work." With their brash verbal attacks, aggressive communicators are more likely to start fights or make conflicts worse.

The way you communicate with others can affect whether conflict occurs and whether a conflict is resolved or gets worse. There is really no "right" way to communicate. Sometimes, the passive approach works best, and other times

An **assertive communicator** responds during arguments with statements like "I understand that this is important to you. It is also important to me. Instead of calling each other names, let's work together and solve the problem."

What Is Your Communication Style?

Read the following questions, and select the A, B, or C answer that is closest to the way you honestly think you would respond to each scenario.

1. While standing in line for tickets at a baseball game, a person ahead of you invites his friend to join him in line. You say:

    A. "Oh, well, there's nothing I can do about it."
    B. "Hey you! Get back to the end of the line!"
    C. "When you jump ahead in line, it's not fair to the rest of us."

2. Your English teacher says that the writing assignment you have submitted is not acceptable, and that it must be redone. You reply:

    A. "I'm an idiot and I never get anything right."
    B. "No way, that's unfair!"
    C. "Okay, but can you explain it again so I can understand what you are looking for?"

3. Something is bothering your friend, and every time you see him he complains about it. Eventually, you start to wish he would talk about something else. The next time he brings up the subject, you say:

    A. "Sure, sure, I understand. Go ahead and talk about what's bothering you."
    B. "Just get over it already! You're really becoming a bore."
    C. "Hey, I understand this has been bothering you, but can you think of something to do about it? I'd be happy to help if I can."

4. In the cafeteria, you put your books on a chair and go to get lunch. When you return with your tray, someone is about to move your books and sit down. Your response is:

    A. "Oh, well, I guess I'll find somewhere else to sit."
    B. "Get your hands off my stuff, you creep!"
    C. "Excuse me, but that's my seat. There's an empty seat across the table if you'd like to sit down with us."

5. A friend is angry because both of you have invited the same girl, Tracy, out on a date. When he confronts you, you say:

    A. "Sorry about that. I can find someone else to ask out."
    B. "Why would Tracy want to go out with you, you jerk?"
    C. "It's up to Tracy who she goes out with. I have the right to ask her if I want to."

6. At a store's checkout counter, you realize that the cashier did not give you the correct change. You tell her about it, but she denies making a mistake. You respond:

    A. "Well, maybe I miscounted. Sorry to bother you."
    B. "Stop lying and give me my money right now, you thief!"
    C. "Look, I'm sure about this. Count the change yourself."

If your answers are mostly As, then your usual communication style is passive. Mostly Bs means that you react aggressively to conflict. Mostly Cs means your preferred communication style is assertive.[1]

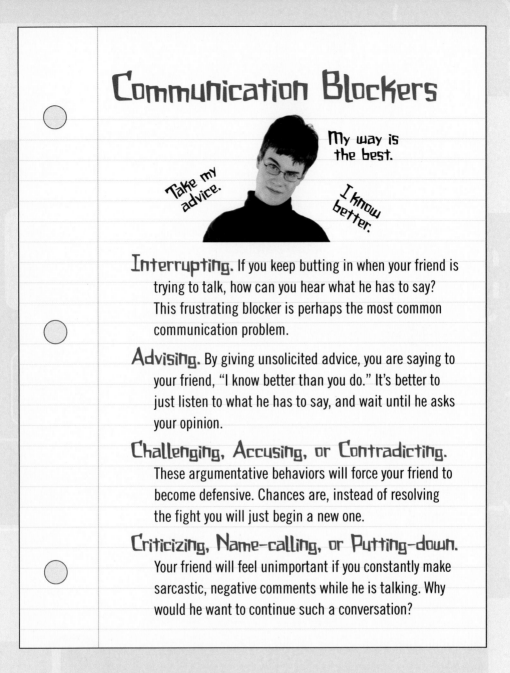

Communication Blockers

Take my advice.

My way is the best.

I know better.

Interrupting. If you keep butting in when your friend is trying to talk, how can you hear what he has to say? This frustrating blocker is perhaps the most common communication problem.

Advising. By giving unsolicited advice, you are saying to your friend, "I know better than you do." It's better to just listen to what he has to say, and wait until he asks your opinion.

Challenging, Accusing, or Contradicting. These argumentative behaviors will force your friend to become defensive. Chances are, instead of resolving the fight you will just begin a new one.

Criticizing, Name-calling, or Putting-down. Your friend will feel unimportant if you constantly make sarcastic, negative comments while he is talking. Why would he want to continue such a conversation?

an aggressive approach is necessary. However, an assertive communication style is usually fair for all concerned.

Assertive communicators know their rights and express their needs and feelings honestly. They insist on being treated fairly. However, at the same time assertive communicators also try to respect and understand others' rights, needs, and

feelings. An assertive communicator is willing to cooperate to find a "win-win" solution.

You can't be an assertive communicator without first being a good listener. In order to be a good listener, you need to focus on what the other person is saying. If all you are thinking about is what you're going to say in response, then you are not really listening—you're preparing for an argument. If you're in the middle of doing something, stop and pay attention while the person is speaking.

Have your conversation in a quiet place where neither of you will be distracted. It may be hard, but control your emotions and let the other person finish speaking instead of interrupting. Allow the person who is speaking as much time as necessary to explain his or her feelings and actions.

When the speaker has finished, you should be able to repeat back, in your own words, his or her complaint. You may not agree with what was said, but if you can repeat the main idea, you will show that you were listening and trying to understand.

Tips for Being a Good Listener

1. Face the speaker and look into his or her eyes.
2. Be relaxed, but pay close attention.
3. As the person speaks, try to feel what he or she is feeling.
4. Don't interrupt.
5. Let the speaker know you are listening by nodding or saying "uh huh."
6. If you don't understand something, wait until the speaker pauses and then ask him or her to explain. ("What do you mean by...?")
7. Keep an open mind.

Solving Conflicts with Friends

Chris borrowed Nick's favorite video game three months ago and didn't return it until last Friday. That night Nick had Chris and several other friends over to his home. He was looking forward to playing the game with them but it wouldn't work. Nick realized the disk had several deep scratches on it. Frowning, he looked at Chris.

"I paid for this game with my own money, and it cost a lot," Nick said. "You better buy me a new one."

"No, " Chris replied. "It worked okay for me. I didn't break it."

"You're lying," Nick insisted. Chris glared at his friend. Then, without saying another word, he stood up and walked out of the house.

Fighting between friends can be very painful, leaving both people feeling a mixture of emotions. Conflict can cause feelings of hurt, betrayal, anger, frustration, and sadness. This was the case with Nick. After Chris left, he felt bad about calling his friend a liar. But he was angry about his broken game. When Nick saw Chris at school the following Monday, he didn't speak to him. The silent treatment lasted a

Guys' Top Five Conflict Starters Between Friends

#%@&!!

#%@&!!

1. Who's right and who's wrong

2. Bragging

3. Who does better at sports or in school

4. The rules of games

5. Insults and name-calling[1]

week, until Nick decided he had to do something. He still wanted to be friends with Chris.

Solving a conflict is a little like solving a math problem—you can't find the solution until you understand the problem. So your first step is to understand what the conflict is all about. Try to calmly evaluate what happened and how your friend's actions made you feel. Ask yourself, is this really important to me? Should I be angry? At the same time, try to understand how your friend feels about what happened. What would it take to resolve your conflict? What would be the most effective way?

The second step—talking things over with the other person—is harder. You may find it difficult to speak with your friend after a fight because you feel embarrassed that the fight occurred in the first place. He or she may feel the same way. In addition, trying to patch things up can sometimes cause another fight. Beginning the conversation with

statements like "You really made me mad last Friday" or "This problem is all your fault" will only make the other person defensive.

One way to prevent further conflict is to share your feelings without attacking or blaming the other person. Instead, you can use carefully worded statements called I-messages.

An I-message has four basic parts:

- "*I feel...*"
  (States how you feel about the issue that caused the conflict.)

- "*...when...*"
  (Gives details about what the other person did or said that caused the hard feelings.)

- "*...because...*"
  (Explains why you feel that way. This can be the hardest part of the I-message.)

- "*I want...*"
  (Describes what you think will resolve the conflict or ease the bad feelings.)

Nick decided to use I-messages the next time he saw Chris at school. "You know," Nick said, "I felt really bad last Friday when the game didn't work because I knew you were the last person to use it. But I want to talk about what happened and try to work things out."

I-messages are solution-oriented statements, expressing feelings and requests.

The Rules of Friendship

Pull your own weight. If one person is always giving in a friendship, the relationship is unbalanced. Support your friend, and expect that person to be there for you as well.

Don't betray a confidence. Trust is an important part of friendship. If your friend tells you a secret, don't tell others.

Beware of criticism. If a friend asks for your opinion, be honest. It is okay to tell a friend when you think he or she is making a mistake. But before you criticize your friend, think about your reasons. Do you mean well, or are you feeling envious?

Acknowledge your friend's success. You may become jealous when your friend wins the wrestling tournament while you were eliminated in the first round. But a strong person can put that jealousy aside and celebrate his friend's success.[2]

Nick's statement addressed the fact that there was a problem, but did not place blame for the fight on Chris. Nick also did not blame himself for the fight. Instead, he acknowledged that there was a problem, and invited his

✔ Steps Toward Conflict Resolution

1. Cool off.
2. Use I-messages to tell what is bothering you.
3. Listen carefully to what the other person has to say.
4. Take responsibility.
5. Brainstorm solutions.
6. Choose a solution and carry it out.

friend to help develop a solution. He also made sure to focus on listening to what Chris had to say.

Chris was able to respond with his own I-message. "I felt angry when you assumed the broken game was my fault, because I knew it wasn't. I saw your little brother throwing the disk around earlier and didn't have a chance to mention it. I felt bad that you called me a liar."

When it was Nick's turn to speak, he restated in his own words what Chris had said. Nick was paraphrasing. This is an active listening strategy—a technique that a person can use in

Brainstorming Steps

1. Determine the problem.
2. Generate as many solutions as possible.
3. Select the best idea.

order to hear and fully understand what another person wants. When you paraphrase, you reword and repeat what someone has just told you. "So, it sounds like I should have given you a chance to explain," Nick admitted.

After you understand where the other person is coming from, you can work together to come up with a solution to a conflict. One way to do this is by brainstorming. That is, you and the other person list all the possible solutions to your conflict. Then determine a solution you agree on.

Both Nick and Chris valued their friendship and wanted it to continue, so they had a fairly easy time coming up with a solution. Nick apologized for hurting his friend's feelings. Chris apologized for taking so long to return the game. He suggested

Good friends will make the effort to resolve conflicts between each other.

that they share the cost of another copy so it wouldn't cost as much to replace.

Not all conflicts among friends are solved as easy as the one between Nick and Chris. Some disagreements may never be fully resolved. This does not have to mean the end of the friendship, although that sometimes happens. However, especially when a conflict is over a minor issue, two people who like and respect each other can "agree to disagree."

When the Group Gets Mad

Sometimes conflicts will involve more than two **people.** You may find yourself pulled in several directions if some of your friends don't like or get along with each other.

Although conflicts involving a group may seem more complex and harder to solve than fights between two friends, you can use the exact same process to resolve disagreements. The first thing to do is to determine what the conflict is about. Is this problem basically a disagreement between two people, while others in the group have taken sides? Are a few people

It can be hard to deal with conflict when it seems like the whole world is against you.

Steps to Solving Group Problems

Stop all blaming. Remember, blaming someone (or even yourself) for a problem will not solve it.

Define the problem. Ask yourself two questions: "What is the problem?" and "Whose problem is it?" If it is not your problem, let the person who "owns" the problem solve it.

Consider asking for help. Once you have thought about the problem, you may want to talk things over with someone else, such as another friend or a trusted adult.

Think of alternative solutions. Brainstorm to come up with as many possible ideas for solving the problem as you can.

Evaluate the alternatives. To determine the best approach, think carefully about how each possible solution will affect you and others.

Make a decision. Choose the alternative that you believe is most likely to succeed, and least likely to hurt anyone.

Follow through. Once you've made a decision, stick to it. However, if after a reasonable amount of time you find things aren't working, try an alternative solution.[1]

The best way to begin to resolve a conflict is to talk about what's causing the problem.

ganging up on someone for some reason? Are you involved because a friend expects you to take a side? Or does this conflict affect you directly?

If you find that you are at the center of a group fight, don't take sides. Instead, try to encourage everyone else to work things out. To do this, you need to determine who is directly involved. Then, spend some time alone with that person—or those people—and talk about what's going on. Listen carefully to figure out what the problem is. Then, explain that you both should brainstorm together to find a solution.

A **confrontation** is a face-to-face encounter or clash involving conflicting ideas or goals.

There are some times, however, when you have to take sides in a group conflict, such as when it involves dangerous or illegal activities. For example, a friend in your group may be using drugs or encouraging others to shoplift. In such cases, you need to be true to yourself and what you believe in. Confront your friend, and explain that what he or she is doing is wrong—and dangerous.

If your friend ignores you, then it is time to tell a parent, teacher, or another trusted adult. This can be very hard—your friend will get into trouble, and you will probably lose his or her trust. But you need to do the right thing. If others in your group are also concerned, ask them to join you when talking to your friend. If necessary, go as a group to tell an adult about the problem.

Even if the group conflict does not involve a serious issue, if the fighting drags on for a long time, it's okay to ask an adult to help resolve the problem. School counselors and teachers usually have had a lot of experience helping groups of kids resolve conflicts and fights just like yours. You might also talk to a parent or to some other trusted adult.

"Peacemaking is not easy. In many ways, it is much more difficult than making war. But its great rewards cannot be measured in ordinary terms."

—Jimmy Carter

"Quit Picking on Me!"

> Since the beginning of the school year Jesse has been bullied in gym class by two larger guys. They constantly tease him, throw his books and papers into the shower, and slap and punch him when no one is looking. Jesse has been too afraid to do anything about it.

Bullying can be physical assaults or verbal abuse—or both. There are many reasons why bullying occurs. Some kids feel a sense of power and control when teasing or harassing their classmates. Others act out as a way to get the attention of their peers. Still others bully to compensate for feelings of inadequacy. They target classmates as a

It can be hard to stand up for yourself, especially if a group is bullying you.

What to Do
If You Are Being Bullied

1. Unless you believe you may be physically harmed, confront your tormentor. Look the bully in the eye and tell him, firmly and clearly, to stop.

2. Get away from the situation as quickly as possible.

3. Tell an adult what has happened immediately. If you are afraid to tell a teacher on your own, ask a friend to go with you.

4. Keep on speaking up until you get someone to listen. Explain what happened, who was involved, where it occurred, and what you have done.

5. Remember, bullying is not your fault—don't blame yourself for what has happened.[1]

way of venting frustration with problems at home or in school. Some people bully because they've been bullied themselves.

Bullies usually torment peers who are weak, unpopular, and unlikely to resist. They often focus on those who are different in some way. Targets can be the new kid who wears the "wrong" clothes, the "teacher's pet," the student with a speech defect or learning disability, or the overweight classmate.

You can be bullied in many different ways. You may be called names, or be pushed, shoved, or hit. You may have your belongings taken or damaged, or be threatened. Bullying may

involve having rumors or gossip spread about you at school or on the Internet.

Bullying is a form of conflict that causes many emotions. If you are the victim of bullying, you probably feel very angry, but also powerless. It's likely that you also feel afraid, especially if you are threatened or physically attacked. You may feel so much anxiety that you'll try to avoid the bullies at any cost: skipping school or staying away from places where you might run into them. You may also feel ashamed at not being able to stand up to the bullies.

You need to recognize that you are not at fault. It is the other person who is behaving in an unacceptable way. No one deserves to be bullied. However, if you are constantly fighting with others or hearing a lot of negative comments from bullies, you can begin to think badly about yourself. This development of low self-esteem can lead to more serious problems, including depression and thoughts of suicide.

Low self-esteem was a problem for one guy who shared his story anonymously on a Web site. He first encountered problems with bullying when in elementary school. Over the

What to Do If You See Someone Being Bullied

Most people are uncomfortable when they see someone being bullied. They often feel guilty because they want to intervene, but don't want the bully to begin targeting or tormenting them. If you see someone being bullied:

1. **Refuse to join in.** It can be hard, but do your best to resist the bully's efforts to get you to tease or torment someone.

2. **If you can, try to defuse the situation.** Try to draw attention away from the person being targeted. If you know the bully, perhaps you can take him aside and ask him to leave the victim alone. However, don't place yourself at risk.

3. **Get help.** Ask a teacher, parent, or other responsible adult to come and help immediately.

4. **Offer support to bullied teens.** Help them up if they have been tripped or knocked down. If you believe you can't do this safely at the time, give words of kindness or condolence later to those who have been hurt.

5. **Encourage the victims to talk with an adult.** Offer to go along if it would help. If the victim of a bully is unwilling to report the incident, tell an adult yourself. (If necessary for your safety, do this anonymously.)[2]

Cyberbullying

A 2004 survey by i-Safe America of fourth through eighth graders reported that 42 percent of them said they had been bullied through the computer—by having personal information or embarrassing photographs of themselves posted online without their knowledge or permission.

Another 35 percent of students said they had been threatened in hostile instant messages or text on Web sites. More than half admitted to having said hurtful things to others online. Almost 60 percent said they did not tell their parents or any other adult about what happened.[3]

years the abuse continued, and he became severely depressed. He explained, "At night I would go into my room and shut the door. I would stay up crying and wishing I were dead. I have tried to kill myself many times. Now I am in high school and

Some of the Symptoms of Depression

- A loss of interest in activities previously enjoyed
- Feelings of worthlessness or guilt
- Fatigue or loss of energy
- Withdrawal from friends and family
- Easily annoyed and frustrated
- Sudden decline in grades
- Appetite or weight changes

nothing has changed. I still want to die but I go to counseling to get help. I wish something [could] be done to stop this."[5]

All young people go through periods of sadness, but deep unhappiness and feelings of hopelessness and despair that last more than a week or two are considered depression. It is an emotional problem that interferes with a teen's ability to function in school and at home.

The Surveys Say...

In 2000, 91 percent of teens said they saw students in their schools get "picked on" during the previous year. Nearly three in ten reported being physically threatened.[4]

If you believe you are affected by depression, get help by talking to someone you trust—a friend, your parents, a school counselor, your family doctor, or a religious leader. The same holds true if you have a friend who seems depressed. Without support, someone suffering from depression is in danger of hurting himself, or possibly taking his own life. The third leading cause of death among fifteen- to twenty-five-year-olds is suicide, and 86 percent of all teenage suicides are boys.[6]

When a Friend May Be Suicidal

If you are concerned about a friend who is threatening suicide or seems suicidal (giving away possessions, avoiding friends, talking about or obsessed with death), talk to a trusted adult or call a suicide prevention hotline. See page 61 for a number to call.

Are You a Bully?

Fourteen-year-old Tucker knows how it feels to be bullied. In school, some of the bigger ninth graders pick on him at lunch. They call him names and sometimes punch him hard in the arm or shoulder. When Tucker gets home, though, he and his friends often tease an eleven-year-old neighborhood boy named Jed. They make fun of Jed's learning disability and call him mean names. "I don't know why I do it," admits Tucker, who feels somewhat guilty and ashamed. "I know how much I hate being teased at school."[1]

Even if you are the victim of a bully, there may be times that you want to bully other kids. Like Tucker, you may not give much thought to your behavior. In fact, Tucker usually tells other people that he is not a bully. He says he is just "fooling around."

Think about how you treat other people—put yourself in their shoes. Ask yourself how you would feel if someone knocked you down or called you names. Chances are, you wouldn't feel very good about it, or about yourself.

Some bullies eventually realize that their behavior is self-destructive, and make an effort to change. They come to recognize that their behavior is not really making them look strong and powerful to others. Instead it makes them appear weak—as well as mean.

If you think you have been acting like a bully and you want to stop, the first step is to talk to the person you've bullied.

Some Myths About Bullying

Myth #1: Bullying is just teasing.

Fact: Bullying is much more than teasing. Bullies may also use violence, threats, or other tactics. When everyone involved considers teasing to be fun, then it can be considered a joke. But bullying hurts.

Myth #2: Some people deserve to be bullied.

Fact: No one deserves to be bullied. Most bullies torment people who are "different" from them, but being different is not a reason to be bullied.

Myth #3: Bullying is a normal part of growing up.

Fact: It is not normal to be pushed around, teased, threatened, insulted, hurt, or abused.

Myth #4: People who are bullied will get over it.

Fact: Bullying hurts for a long time. Some victims of bullies drop out of school because of their fear. Some become depressed or even commit suicide. If you ask an adult, chances are he or she will remember being bullied. People don't "get over" being bullied easily.[2]

Apologize for your past behavior. Then, the next time you see that person, make an effort to have something good to say. To stop yourself from being a bully you need to recognize that you are placing your own anger and other negative emotions on your victim. And that behavior is not healthy for either of you. If you think you need help to change your ways, you might want to talk to your parents or to a school counselor.

"You must be the change you want to see in the world."

—Mohandas K. Gandhi

Are You a Bully?

When Peers Help Solve Problems

> Jake accidentally bumped into Shawn in the hallway, causing him to stumble and fall. "Hey, you!" Shawn yelled. "Watch where you're going, you idiot."
>
> Jake was tired of Shawn's attitude. For the past couple of weeks, Shawn had found every opportunity to insult Jake, criticizing him and calling him names in the hallways and lunchroom, and during recess. "Oh, shut up," he retorted. "No one cares what you think."
>
> As Shawn and Jake stared angrily at each other, a crowd of students began to gather. "Hold everything," another student called out, as he stepped between the two. "Seems like you both need to go to peer mediation."

Sometimes, two people get into a disagreement that they are unable to resolve on their own. If they are lucky, their school may have a program that helps with conflicts. In peer mediation programs, students

> " When you talk it out, like when you can sit down and talk about it, you're not as mad. That's the way I see it. When you start talkin' about it, the anger just dies down. You just become more civilized; you go back into your regular state of mind.
> —Student helped by peer mediation[1] "

Sometimes, a third person can step in and offer a new viewpoint.

who are involved in a dispute take their problem to a neutral third party, or mediator. The peer mediator is also a student. He or she doesn't take sides in the conflict but tries to help find a "win-win" solution to the problem.

When two people submit their argument for peer mediation, they must agree to follow the program's ground rules and

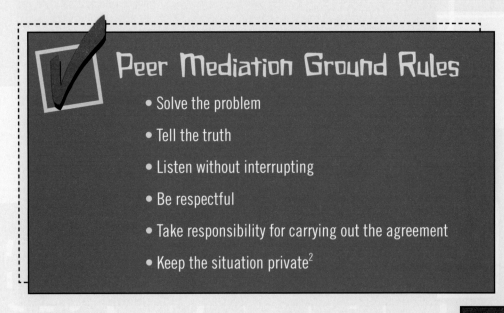

Peer Mediation Ground Rules

- Solve the problem
- Tell the truth
- Listen without interrupting
- Be respectful
- Take responsibility for carrying out the agreement
- Keep the situation private[2]

When Peers Help Solve Problems

Most Frequent Reasons for Mediation

- Rumors
- Name-calling
- Put-downs
- Boyfriend/girlfriend issues
- Threats
- Lost or damaged property

steps. Then the peer mediator works with them to define the problem. First, one person is given a chance to speak, and then the other tells his or her side of the story. The mediator can ask questions to clarify things. When they are finished, sometimes the mediator will ask each party to repeat the other's story, to show that both points of view are clearly understood.

The next step is for each of the parties involved to suggest ways to resolve the part of the problem that he or she is responsible for. This will show areas where each side might be willing to compromise.

Finally, both parties brainstorm possible solutions to their problem. Each solution should be discussed and evaluated. Eventually, both parties will agree to a solution (or, in some cases, a combination of solutions). This agreement must be

> We help kids who are fighting talk about their problems. Some people think kids can't help other kids solve their problems. But we can. It's real neat because we don't work out things for kids who are fighting. They solve their own problems and we help.
>
> —Student peer mediator [3]

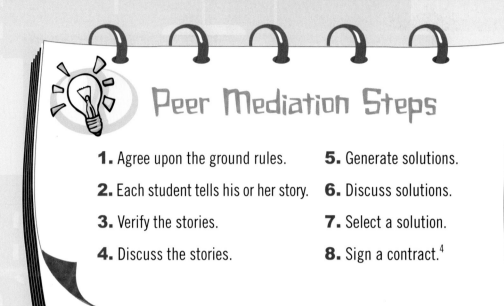

Peer Mediation Steps

1. Agree upon the ground rules.
2. Each student tells his or her story.
3. Verify the stories.
4. Discuss the stories.
5. Generate solutions.
6. Discuss solutions.
7. Select a solution.
8. Sign a contract.[4]

done freely—if one person is pressured into accepting a solution, the mediation process will probably not work out.

The agreed-upon solution is then written down as a contract, which all participants sign. It usually consists of a simple statement such as "I will stop calling Michael names if he will stop calling me names."

Today, thousands of elementary, middle, and high schools across the nation make use of peer mediation programs. School administrators believe they help reduce incidents of violence, absences, and suspensions. But such programs also provide students with the chance to talk to their peers about issues they might have a hard time bringing up with an adult.

Peer mediation is not really about deciding who is right and who is wrong in a particular argument. Instead, the process is meant to help students learn how to move beyond the immediate conflict, resolve problems peacefully, and get along better with each other.

Conflicts with Adults

Derek thinks his history teacher doesn't like him. Yesterday, when he left his seat to sharpen his pencil, Mrs. Spellman yelled at him and told him that he had just earned a detention. Later, when students were talking during class, she sent Derek to the principal's office. He felt the punishment wasn't fair, because he wasn't the one doing most of the talking. And this wasn't the first time that he thought his teacher was punishing him for things he didn't do.

At times, everyone gets into disagreements with people who are not their peers: parents, teachers, or other adults. If you were in Derek's position, what would you do?

Well, just like you do with peer conflicts, you need to take some time and think about the cause of this particular kind of conflict. Is the teacher angry about something you are doing or because you are not trying hard in class? If so, perhaps if you change your behavior the situation will improve.

Does your teacher seem to have a personal grudge against you, or does he or she appear to treat everyone unfairly? Answer this question

Conflict with a coach can be frustrating. Take action to end it by explaining your side of the story.

honestly—maybe you are being oversensitive. Teachers are human, too (believe it or not!). Just like you, they can get annoyed and angry and sometimes take out their frustration on others unfairly.

Your first step in resolving an issue with your teacher is to ask him or her if you could meet to discuss your problem. When you meet, remain calm and respectful as you outline your concerns.

Resolving Conflict Through Negotiation

1. Agree to negotiate.
2. Gather points of view.
3. Focus on interests.
4. Create win-win solutions.
5. Evaluate solutions.
6. Create an agreement.[1]

If you decide that there really is a problem between you and an adult, it's probably better not to confront the adult yourself. If you accuse your teacher of hating you, saying so may make things worse instead of better. In fact, he or she may think you are the one being unfair and looking to start an argument.

Get other adults to help you—tell your parents about the situation and ask for their advice. Be honest about what is going on and tell the whole story. Your parents may have good advice on how to deal with the problem, or they may want to step in and make sure it is resolved.

In Derek's case, after he told his mother about the problem in history class, she scheduled a meeting with his teacher,

The word **negotiation** means reaching an agreement through discussion and compromise.

Differing Perspectives

As with all conflicts, the reasons for disagreements between young people and adults can vary. Poor communication and lack of respect often play a large part. Sometimes, young people do not think about how their behavior affects other people. At the same time, adults may unfairly mistrust young people or have negative attitudes toward them.

Consider, for example, the conflict that develops between a shopkeeper and a group of teenagers who spend hours at a time hanging out in front of his store. The kids are surprised and upset when the store owner tells them to leave. From their perspective, they are not bothering anyone. They are just having fun together.

The shopkeeper, however, has a different perspective. In the past, he has had problems with kids hassling customers and stealing things. Also, the group of kids is loud and boisterous, and he is worried that they may be scaring customers away.

To resolve this conflict, both sides need to meet so they can negotiate and brainstorm ideas to solve their conflict. Possible solutions? The shopkeeper could permit the teens to sit in front of his store only during certain times of the day. The kids could promise to be quieter and not block the entrance or annoy customers.

Mrs. Spellman. At the meeting, Derek's mom did not accuse the teacher of mistreating her son. She simply asked to talk about the situation. Derek's mother learned that Mrs. Spellman was having a hard time with several troublemakers in her class, and that Derek was often caught in the middle. Derek's mother then scheduled a second meeting with Mrs. Spellman and a

vice principal at the school. The vice principal agreed to sit in on the class; if things didn't get better, Derek would be moved to a different class.

Obviously, every conflict involving adults or non-peers will have different causes and issues. The important thing is not to panic or get angry. Many of the same strategies used to resolve conflicts with peers can be used to solve problems with family members or adults.

✔ Tips for Talking to Adults

Bring up your issue when the adult has the time to listen. Don't try to talk when they're busy with something else. Say, "Is this a good time for you? I have something important to discuss."

Be aware of your body language. Don't roll your eyes, cross your arms, or clench your fists. Look the other person in the eyes and try to remain calm.

Use respectful language. Don't use sarcasm, insults, or put-downs when explaining your point of view. Snapping something like, "That's a stupid reason," will only make the other person angry.

Be honest. Tell the truth about how you feel or what has happened.

Listen to the other side of the issue. The adult will be more likely to show you the same respect.

State your case using "I-messages." "I felt upset when I got detention because I wasn't talking in class. I want you to understand what really happened."

Fighting with Your Siblings

Did you know that it is common for baby great white sharks to eat each other? When the first sharks hatch inside the mother's body, they get additional nourishment by eating most of the unhatched eggs. Of the approximately sixty eggs that the female great white produces, sometimes only two or three will be born. Somehow, the young sharks instinctively know that their best chance for survival comes by eliminating their brothers and sisters, who would otherwise compete for their food.

The word *competition* is used to describe a struggle for limited resources, such as food. It can also be used to describe a contest in which two or more people seek the same goal. Another word that is sometimes used to describe an intense competition between two people is *rivalry*. When brothers or sisters argue among themselves, it is known as sibling rivalry.

Chances are, you don't fight with your brothers to decide which of you will get to eat dinner. But most family fights do involve a limited resource—the love and attention of your parents. If one

Quarterback Sibling Rivalry

A little competition between siblings is often considered a good thing. But sibling rivalry reached new levels on September 10, 2006, when thirty-year-old Peyton Manning (of the Indianapolis Colts) and twenty-five-year-old Eli Manning (of the New York Giants) became the first brothers to start at quarterback in the same NFL game (Eli's Giants lost to Peyton's Colts).

In general, the brothers try to keep professional competition from affecting their family relationship. In fact, Peyton is very supportive of his brother although he rarely has the chance to see Eli's games. "I enjoy watching him play on the highlights," Peyton says, "and to watch him play in person is a real treat."[1]

sibling feels that he or she is not getting enough attention, he or she is going to feel jealous of other family members.

You might feel jealous, for example, if your parents get very excited about something your older brother has done, such as getting good grades or winning a sports award. Even though you're probably also proud of him, you may feel hurt, particularly if you think that your parents never made an equally big fuss over something you did.

Jealousy is often accompanied by strong emotions, such as anger and frustration. Siblings often express these feelings by fighting with each other, which makes things worse. If you get

Beating the Green-Eyed Monster!

Jealousy is one of the most common emotions.
It doesn't matter how old you are, or how rich and famous—everyone struggles with jealousy sometimes. Until you learn how to handle this "Green-Eyed Monster," life is going to be pretty miserable.

To deal with feelings of jealousy, try to forget about the other person and think about yourself. That is, instead of concentrating on what your sibling has or what he or she does, think about all the things that you have and who you are. For example, you may feel jealous because your brother won a prize for his drawing, but perhaps you are better at something else: sports, or math, or writing. If your parents give your sister a new bike, think about the special things your parents have given to you. Chances are, your parents are not trying to favor either of you.

Feelings of jealousy may not go away until you let them out. You may want to write down what you are feeling, or talk privately with one of your parents or family members. If you try to hold in your feelings, they will eventually boil over into frustration and anger. Expressing your feelings will help your jealousy go away—at least a little bit—and you'll feel better.

in trouble for starting a fight, you're going to feel even angrier and more frustrated. Or, once the fight is over, you may feel guilty for having upset your brother or sister.

You'll feel better about yourself if you can keep your temper when you recognize that you are feeling jealous, angry, or frustrated. It may help to leave the room and think about things for a few minutes. Has your sibling really done something that should make you angry? Or are you just

frustrated with the situation? You may find that you're not even really upset at your brother or sister, but just want to take out your frustration on someone.

Tips for Getting Along with Brothers and Sisters

Spend some time together. Invite your younger sister to play a board game with you. Ask your older brother to kick the soccer ball around. If you spend a little time together, you can understand what he or she is thinking.

Go out of your way to give your brother or sister a compliment. Positive communication is key to building a strong, healthy relationship.

Show an interest in your sibling's hobbies and interests. Attend his or her sporting events, dance recitals, and other activities. Share your own hobbies and interests, too.

Pick your battles. If your sibling did something deliberately to hurt you, then you need to confront him or her. But nothing good results from getting mad if your brother or sister broke something of yours accidentally.

If you find yourself becoming irritated over something your sibling has done, take time to cool down. Walk away from the situation. Take a deep breath and count to ten. When you can think more calmly, come back and talk things out using a calm, quiet voice.

Fighting with Your Parents

> Doug had made plans to go to the movies on Saturday afternoon with his friend Kyle. But on Saturday morning, Doug's parents announced that the family was going to spend the day cleaning up the house and doing yard work. Doug was very angry. He had done his chores all week and was looking forward to time for himself. Why were his parents being so unfair?

Like Doug, you may sometimes feel like your parents' rules are unreasonable. However, when parents establish rules it is usually because they have your best interests in mind.

For many years, your parents' most important job has been watching out for you. When you were very young, your parents made almost all of the decisions that affected you— what you ate, what clothes you wore, and how you spent your time. As you grow older and become more independent, your parents may find it hard to "let go" and allow you to make your own choices. At the same time, they may be asking you to give up some of your time in order to help out at home.

Chores can be a source of conflict with parents.

One way to avoid conflict with your parents is to talk with them regularly. Tell them how you feel about their rules. And let them know your opinions. Be honest. How can your parents understand what you are thinking and feeling if you don't tell them?

If your parents establish a rule that you happen to think is unfair—a curfew, a time limit on Internet use, or a demand that you cut your hair or wear different clothes—don't

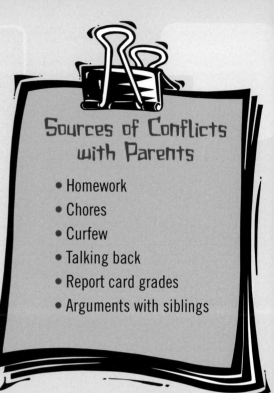

Sources of Conflicts with Parents

- Homework
- Chores
- Curfew
- Talking back
- Report card grades
- Arguments with siblings

scream or yell at them. You'll have better luck if you clearly and calmly explain why you feel their rule is unfair. Make sure you have their complete attention when you are talking to them. When you are finished, ask them to explain why they feel such a restriction is important or necessary, and listen carefully to their reasons. They may have good reasons that you had not considered.

If you want greater freedom, it might help to show your parents that you are willing to take on more responsibility. Perhaps together you can work out a compromise. Offer to do additional chores if they will let you go to a concert with your friends, watch a particular television program, or stay out an hour later on a Friday night.

In Doug's case, he didn't argue with his parents. He calmly explained to them that he had already made plans for the afternoon. He said that he would be happy to work around the house in the morning, and promised to do whatever

work was left on Sunday afternoon. When he was finished talking, his parents agreed to let him go to the movies. They acknowledged that Doug was good about doing his chores—a sign of responsibility—and they had not known that he had already made plans.

Sometimes your parents might not be willing to compromise or change their minds. In those cases, you will have to abide by their decision, even though you feel it is unfair. But if you continue to show your parents that you are responsible, they are more likely to be willing to give you greater freedom.

Sometimes you may have a conflict over how to handle arguments your parents are having with each other. Some may be about little things, like doing chores, weekend plans, or what's for dinner. Or arguments may be about bigger things, like family finances.

It can be difficult to deal with parents when they don't get along with each other and fight frequently.

Conflict

Crisis Hotlines

If you believe a friend or family member is in danger because of violence at home, pick up the phone and call a crisis hotline. The number for the National Domestic Violence Hotline appears on page 61.

When your parents disagree, you may feel worried, sad, or upset. But it's important to keep in mind that arguments usually do not mean parents don't love each other, or that they're going to get a divorce. Everyone loses his or her temper occasionally. Even if the argument is about you, remember that it is not your fault.

Sometimes arguments can become unpleasant. Parents may yell and scream, call each other names, and say nasty things to each other. If this happens, you may feel that you have to become involved. The best approach is to wait until the shouting has ended, and your parents have cooled down. Then, talk to them individually. Without blaming anyone, tell your parents how their arguments make you feel. That thought may help them control their tempers the next time they become angry with each other.

In a few cases, arguments get out of control and parents throw things or hit each other. This type of behavior is never okay. You need to let another adult know what is going on. Talk to close relatives, a teacher, a school counselor, or a trusted family friend. That adult may be able to speak with your parents or help them get counseling.

You're Not Alone

> Trey is in his first year at a large middle school, and he doesn't know many people. Every morning during homeroom, the two guys seated behind him make mean and insulting comments about him. They're speaking too low for the teacher to hear. Derrick—the guy sitting next to Trey—is friendly most of the time. But when the guys behind Trey start teasing him, Derrick doesn't say anything. Trey doesn't want to fight or tell the teacher. He's feeling angry, frustrated, and anxious, but most of all he is feeling isolated because of this conflict.

Trey is not alone—everyone experiences some conflict practically every day. Conflict causes stress and can damage or destroy relationships if it is not managed properly. That's why it is so important for young people to understand how to deal with the conflicts in their lives.

If you are feeling upset about a conflict, it may be helpful to remember that conflict is normal. Talk to your parents or another trusted adult—chances are, they will be able to tell you stories about conflicts or bullying that happened to them when they were your age. Ask your friends to share their stories, and you'll find that they are probably similar to yours.

Conflict can make you feel isolated and alone.

The basic steps to resolving conflict are the same in all cases. First, you need to understand exactly what the issue is. Also, think about your own feelings about the conflict, because that will help you to control your emotions more easily.

The next step is to address the conflict. This may involve confronting another person, but should be done without blaming them for causing the problem. Then listen to their point of view, and try to empathize with their perspective.

Next, you should be able to work together to generate ideas that will help you manage or resolve the conflict. Try to be creative—most people can only think of two ways—fighting or ignoring the problem. Once you've come up with a solution that is acceptable to both parties, put it into practice.

Empathy is the ability to identify with another person, and to understand his or her feelings and attitudes.

☑ Take Charge of Your Anger

When anger goes unmanaged, it can add fuel to the fire and make conflict worse. As one negative thought leads to another, anger increases and the conflict grows in size.

In Trey's case, after thinking about the problem he approached one of the bullies at his locker between periods. "I want to talk to you," he said. "I have a problem with how you talk about me in homeroom. I don't understand what I did to get picked on. I want the teasing to stop, and I'd prefer to work things out in a friendly way, rather than by telling a teacher and maybe getting us both into trouble."

Trey had been nervous about approaching the other guy, but the bully seemed to be listening. Although there was no formal

Be assertive and creative when dealing with conflict.

agreement that the teasing would end, Trey felt better about himself. During the last homeroom period of the day before the end of school, the guys behind him were quiet. When Derrick cracked a joke about the upcoming school dance, Trey joined in. School didn't seem so bad after all, he thought.

Trey's story shows how if you are assertive and deal with a problem you can eliminate it. If you take the time to understand conflict and know the steps needed to deal with it, you will be able to reduce the stress, anger, and anxiety in your life.

Controlling Your Anger

Avoid losing control.

Never use your body or words to hurt others.

Get away from the situation if you feel overwhelmed.

Evaluate your choices about what to do next.

Remember that you are responsible for your choices. You can choose whether or not to let a situation make you angry. [2]

"Nothing builds self-esteem and self-confidence like accomplishment."

—Thomas Carlyle

Chapter 2. How Conflict Makes You Feel

1. Carroll E. Izard, *The Psychology of Emotions* (New York: Plenum Press, 1991), p. 248.

Chapter 3. Finding Solutions

1. Naomi Drew, *The Kids Guide to Working Out Conflicts: How to Keep Cool, Stay Safe, and Get Along* (Minneapolis, Minn.: Free Spirit Publishing, 2004), p. 14.

2. H. S. Ross and C. L. Conant, "The Social Structure of Early Conflict: Interaction, Relationships, and Alliances," in C. Shantz & W. Hartup, eds., *Conflict in Child and Adolescent Development* (Cambridge, England: Cambridge University Press, 1992), p. 156.

Chapter 4. Effective Communication

1. David Cowan, Susanna Palomares, and Dianne Schilling, *Conflict Resolution Skills for Teens* (Spring Valley, Calif.: Innerchoice Publishing, 1994), pp. 89–90.

Chapter 5. Solving Conflicts with Friends

1. Drew, p. 7.

2. Adapted from Florence Isaacs, *Toxic Friends, True Friends: How Your Friends Can Make or Break Your Health, Happiness, Family, and Career* (New York: William Morrow, 1999), pp. 220–225.

Chapter 6. When the Group Gets Mad

1. Adapted from Cowan et al., pp. 51–54.

Chapter 7. "Quit Picking on Me!"

1. Adapted from Dorothea M. Ross, *Childhood Bullying and Teasing: What School Personnel, Other Professionals, and Parents Can Do* (Alexandria, Va.: American Counseling Association, 2003), p. 93.

2. Adapted from i-Safe America, "Cyber Bullying: Statistics and Tips," n.d., <http://www.isafe.org/channels/sub.php?ch=op &sub_id=media_cyber_bullying> (March 27, 2007).

3. Adapted from the National Youth Violence Prevention Resource Center, "Bullying," n.d., <http://www.safeyouth.org/ scripts/teens/bullying.asp> (March 7, 2007).

4. USA Weekend.com, "Special Reports: Teens & Safety," April 16, 2000, <http://www.usaweekend.com/00_issues/ 000416/000416teen.html> (March 7, 2007).

5. JaredStory.com, "Dacia's Homework Assignment," n.d., <http://www.jaredstory.com/dacias_homework.html> (March 7, 2007).

6. U.S. Centers for Disease Control, "Suicide: Fact Sheet," n.d., <http://www.cdc.gov/ncipc/factsheets/suifacts.htm> (March 7, 2007).

Chapter 8. Are You a Bully?

1. Personal interview with Tucker, April 2006.

2. Adapted from Pamela Espeland, *Life Lists for Teens: Tips, Steps, Hints, and How-tos for Growing up, Getting Along, Learning, and Having Fun* (Minneapolis, Minn.: Free Spirit Publishing, 2003), p. 94.

Chapter 9. When Peers Help Solve Problems

1. From Donna Crawford and Richard Bodine, *Conflict Resolution Education: A Guide to Implementing Programs in Schools, Youth-Serving Organizations, and Community and Juvenile Justice Settings* (Washington, D.C.: Office of Juvenile Justice and Delinquency Prevention, U.S. Department of Justice, October 1996), p. 44.

2. Adapted from Teacher Talk, "Peer Mediation," June 30, 1997, <http://education.indiana.edu/cas/tt/v2i3/peer.html> (March 7, 2007).

3. Crawford and Bodine, p. 44.

4. Adapted from Teacher Talk.

Chapter 10. Conflicts with Adults

1. Adapted from Crawford and Bodine, Appendix pp. I-1–I-3.

Chapter 11. Fighting with Your Siblings

1. Ken Palmer, "Peyton on Hand to Support Little Brother," *The Giant Insider*, October 15, 2006, <http://giants.scout.com/2/579636.html> (March 7, 2007).

Chapter 13. You're Not Alone

1. Adapted from Espeland, p. 61.

2. Adapted from U.S. Centers for Disease Control, "Bam! Guide to Getting Along: Cool Rules," *BAM! Body and Mind*, n.d., <http://www.bam.gov/sub_yourlife/yourlife_conflict_3.html> (March 7, 2007).

active listening—A technique in which the listener focuses intently on hearing and understanding what another person is saying.

anger—A strong emotion characterized by feelings of annoyance.

anxiety—Feelings of nervousness or agitation about something that is about to happen.

brainstorming—To come up with a variety of solutions to a problem.

conflict—A disagreement caused by differences in ideas, principles, hopes, expectations, or feelings.

contempt—A feeling that someone or something is inferior, or does not deserve respect.

disgust—Feelings of horrified distaste for someone or something.

empathy—The ability to identify with and understand another person's feelings or perspective.

guilt—A feeling of being responsible for wrongdoing, often accompanied by feelings of shame and regret.

I-message—A statement using the word "I" that helps someone to understand how the speaker is feeling, without blaming the other person.

mediator—A person who doesn't take sides in a conflict, but helps bring about its resolution.

negotiate—To make an agreement through discussion and compromise.

paraphrasing—An active listening strategy in which you reword and repeat what someone has just told you.

sadness—A powerful emotion, characterized by feelings of unhappiness, grief, or sorrow.

self-esteem—A person's confidence in his or her worth or merit.

shame—A negative emotion that combines feelings of unworthiness, grief, or sorrow.

sibling rivalry—Competition between brothers and sisters.

FURTHER READING

Drew, Naomi. *The Kids' Guide to Working Out Conflicts.* Minneapolis, Minn.: Free Spirit Publishing, 2004.

Judson, Karen. *Resolving Conflicts: How to Get Along When You Don't Get Along.* Berkeley Heights, N.J.: Enslow Publishers, Inc., 2005.

Verdick, Elizabeth. *How to Take the Grrr Out of Anger.* Minneapolis, Minn.: Free Spirit Publishing, 2002.

Wilde, Jerry. *More Hot Stuff to Help Kids Chill Out: The Anger and Stress Management Book.* Richmond, Ind.: LGR Productions, 2001.

INTERNET ADDRESSES

BAM! Guide to Getting Along
http://www.bam.gov/sub_yourlife/yourlife_conflict.html

Dealing with Feelings
http://kidshealth.org/kid/feeling/index.html

It's My Life
http://pbskids.org/itsmylife/index.html

HOTLINE TELEPHONE NUMBERS

National Domestic Violence Hotline
1-800-799-SAFE (1-800-799-7233)

National Suicide Prevention Lifeline
1-800-273-TALK (1-800-273-8255)

CONTRIBUTORS

Author **Jim Gallagher** has written more than 20 books for young readers. He lives outside Philadelphia, Pennsylvania.

Series advisor **Dr. Carroll Izard,** is the Trustees Distinguished Professor of Psychology at the University of Delaware. His research and writing focuses on the development of emotion knowledge and emotion regulation and their contributions to social and emotional competence. He is author or editor of seventeen books (one of which won a national award) and more than one hundred articles in scientific journals. Dr. Izard is a fellow of both national psychological associations and the American Association for the Advancement of Science. He is the winner of the American Psychological Association's G. Stanley Hall Award and an international exchange fellowship from the National Academy of Sciences.

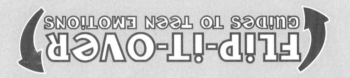

FLiP-iT-OVER
GUiDES TO TEEN EMOTiONS

A Guys' Guide to Anger; A Girls' Guide to Anger
ISBN-13: 978-0-7660-2853-1   ISBN-10: 0-7660-2853-4

A Guys' Guide to Conflict; A Girls' Guide to Conflict
ISBN-13: 978-0-7660-2852-4   ISBN-10: 0-7660-2852-6

A Guys' Guide to Jealousy; A Girls' Guide to Jealousy
ISBN-13: 978-0-7660-2854-8   ISBN-10: 0-7660-2854-2

A Guys' Guide to Loneliness; A Girls' Guide to Loneliness
ISBN-13: 978-0-7660-2856-2   ISBN-10: 0-7660-2856-9

A Guys' Guide to Love; A Girls' Guide to Love
ISBN-13: 978-0-7660-2855-5   ISBN-10: 0-7660-2855-0

A Guys' Guide to Stress; A Girls' Guide to Stress
ISBN-13: 978-0-7660-2857-9   ISBN-10: 0-7660-2857-7

GIRLS!

STOP

Boring Guys' Stuff
From This Point On!